REGENT'S PARK

AND PRIMROSE HILL

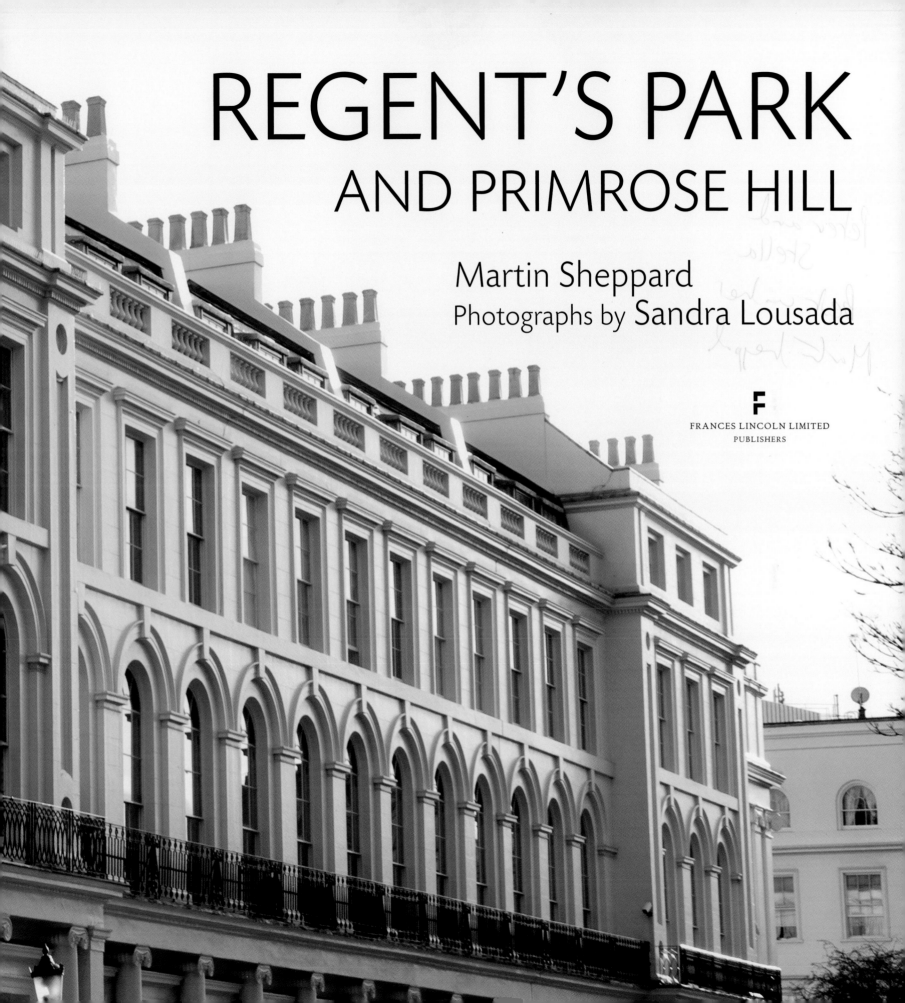

REGENT'S PARK

AND PRIMROSE HILL

Martin Sheppard

Photographs by Sandra Lousada

FRANCES LINCOLN LIMITED
PUBLISHERS

To my mother
and to
the memory
of my father

*Peter and
Stella
Best wisher
Martin Sheppard*

Frances Lincoln Ltd
4 Torriano Mews
Torriano Avenue
London NW5 2RZ
www.franceslincoln.com

HALF-TITLE PAGE Greylag goose.

TITLE PAGE Park Square East (1823)
houses the headquarters of the
Prince's Trust.

RIGHT Autumn in Regent's Park.

CONTENTS

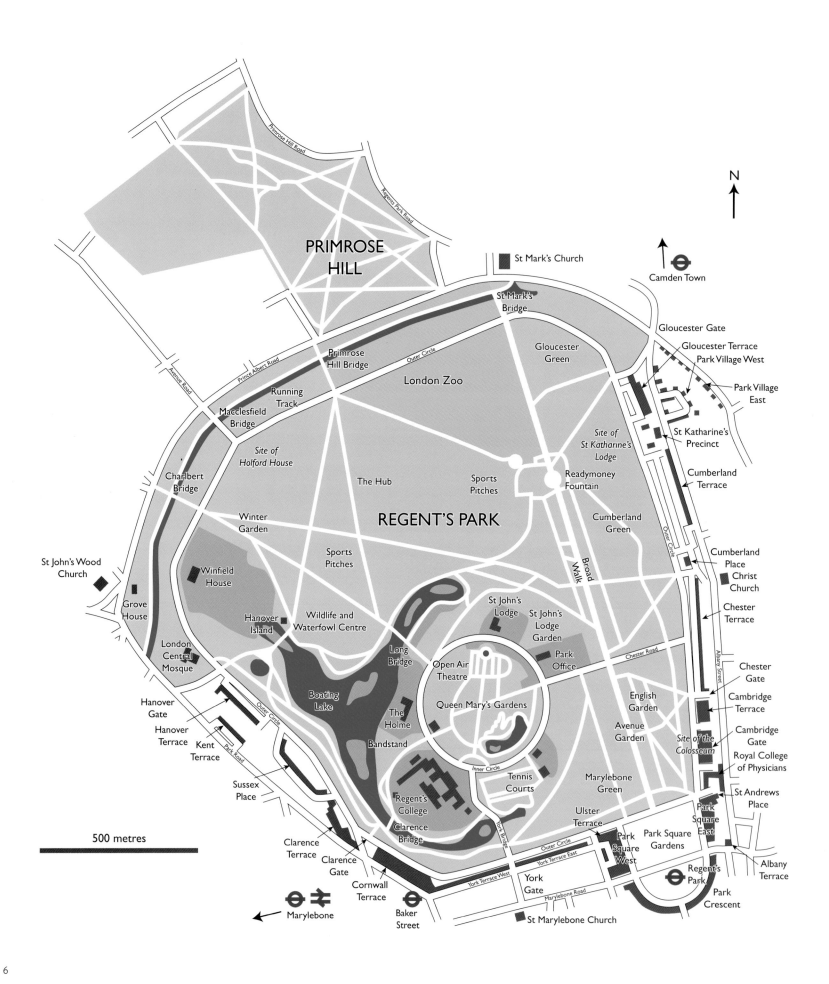

N

PRIMROSE HILL

St Mark's Church

Camden Town

St Mark's Bridge

Primrose Hill Road

Regents Park Road

Prince Albert Road

Primrose Hill Bridge

Outer Circle

Gloucester Green

London Zoo

Gloucester Gate

Gloucester Terrace
Park Village West

Park Village East

Running Track

Macclesfield Bridge

Site of Holford House

Site of St Katharine's Lodge

St Katharine's Precinct

Avenue Road

Charlbert Bridge

The Hub

Sports Pitches

Readymoney Fountain

Cumberland Terrace

REGENT'S PARK

Cumberland Green

Winter Garden

Cumberland Place

Christ Church

St John's Wood Church

Winfield House

Sports Pitches

Broad Walk

Outer Circle

Chester Terrace

Grove House

Hanover Island

Wildlife and Waterfowl Centre

St John's Lodge

St John's Lodge Garden

Chester Road

Albany Street

Chester Gate

London Central Mosque

Long Bridge

Open Air Theatre

Park Office

English Garden

Cambridge Terrace

Hanover Gate

Boating Lake

The Holme

Queen Mary's Gardens

Avenue Garden

Cambridge Gate

Site of the Colosseum

Royal College of Physicians

Hanover Terrace

Kent Terrace

Outer Circle

Park Road

Bandstand

Inner Circle

Tennis Courts

Marylebone Green

St Andrews Place

Sussex Place

Regent's College

Clarence Bridge

York Bridge

Ulster Terrace

Park Square East

500 metres

Clarence Terrace

Clarence Gate

Cornwall Terrace

Baker Street

York Gate

Park Square West

Outer Circle

York Terrace East

Park Square Gardens

Albany Terrace

Regent's Park

Marylebone

York Terrace West

Marylebone Road

Park Crescent

St Marylebone Church

INTRODUCTION

London has six royal parks in or near its centre, green oases in the middle of the city. Two of these parks are relatively small: St James's Park and Green Park lie at the heart of the British establishment, divided from each other by the Mall and bordered by Whitehall, St James's Palace, Buckingham Palace and Piccadilly. Hyde Park is much larger. A royal park from the time of the Reformation, it was opened to the public by Charles I in 1637 and became the favourite parade of fashionable society. To its west, Kensington Gardens were laid out in the years after 1720.

These parks, added to the much older park around the royal palace of Greenwich dating from 1433, were established before London had begun most of its massive outward growth. The sixth of the inner city's royal parks, the Regent's Park, was not created until the early nineteenth century, when the tide of building started to burst London's boundaries. Its principal architect was John Nash, who linked the park, via the new artery of Regent Street, to St James's Park and Westminster. Named after the Prince Regent, Regent's Park was part of the most impressive exercise in town planning in English history. To its immediate north, Primrose Hill, with its superb views over London, was added as a separate but integrally linked park in 1842.

Cherry blossom. Regent's Park has fine displays of cherries along Chester Road and at the southern end of the Avenue Garden.

1

A ROYAL PARK

In 1526 Henry VIII fell in love with Anne Boleyn. Anne's insistence on being queen rather than just the king's mistress, and the unwillingness of Pope Clement VII to sanction the annulment of Henry's marriage to Catherine of Aragon, led to England's break with Rome and to the English Reformation. Henry gained not only his divorce, and Anne, but also the entire lands and property of the monasteries. Among the monastic lands was an estate, belonging to Westminster Abbey, which became Hyde Park. Another, in the manor of Tyburn, which had belonged to Barking Abbey since before the Norman Conquest, became the core of Marylebone Park. Nearly three hundred years later, this in turn became Regent's Park.

Marylebone Park, a roughly circular area of 554 acres not based on previous manorial boundaries, which also included land taken or bought from other owners, offered Henry the convenience of an extra hunting park – in addition to Hyde Park – near to London. Established in 1538, it took its name from St Mary le Bourne, a church by the River Tyburn or Tybourne in the village of Marybone or Marylebone. The new park's land was part of the ancient Middlesex Forest, lying mainly on clay and at a distance from both London and Westminster. The difficulties of draining the land, and of water supply, meant that it had always been lightly inhabited.

The park was soon surrounded by a ring mound, later topped with fencing, to keep in the deer to be hunted for the king's pleasure, with ponds dug along the Tyburn for their water and lodges for their keepers. To its south, near the church, was a manor house. Henry's successors, including Elizabeth I, his daughter by Anne Boleyn, continued to use Marylebone Park for hunting, as did James I, the first Stuart king of England, a passionate huntsman. James's son, Charles I, was less interested in hunting. From 1640, moreover, Charles was preoccupied with political and later military problems, his dispute with the Long Parliament culminating in the English Civil War.

Desperate to raise money for the war, Charles granted the lease on the park to two of his supporters, Sir George Strode and John Wandesford, in return for gunpowder; but Parliament's hold on London prevented them from enjoying the lease and Charles's defeat led to their exile. Following Charles's execution, on 30 January 1649, the monarchy was abolished and all royal assets, including Charles's lands (and his superb art collection) were confiscated and sold. Marylebone Park, which contained three lodges, a hunting stand, stables and orchards, as well as 124 deer and 16,297 trees, predominantly oak, ash, elm, whitethorn and maple, was sold off by sealed tender, for £13,215 6s. 8d., to pay off the arrears of the parliamentary regiments. Almost half of it came into the hands of the cavalry commander and regicide Colonel Thomas Harrison. Uncertain of the future, he and the other new owners made sure of an immediate profit by subletting and by wholesale tree felling. While most of the timber was sold for private gain, 2805 trees in the park were reserved for Cromwell's active and highly successful navy. In 1651, the deer were moved to St James's Park.

On his Restoration in 1660, Charles II granted the lease of Marylebone Park to one of his supporters in exile, Sir Henry Bennet, later the Earl of Arlington, and Strode and Wandesford were grudgingly compensated. Eight years later, it was disparked, ending its status as a hunting preserve. For the next 150 years the park was used as farmland, the main leases passing between a series of aristocrats and bankers, who let the land to tenant farmers. The growing population of London provided a ready market for the park's dairy products, especially milk, as it did for the fodder needed for the ever-increasing number of horses stabled in the capital. In the southern part of the park, the soil was also used for brick-making.

In the eighteenth century the village of Marylebone, previously separate from London and best known for its pleasure gardens, began to grow as it was developed by Edward Harley, Earl of Oxford, its principal landowner.

The magnificent wrought-iron gates at the main entrance to Queen Mary's Gardens, celebrating the Silver Jubilee of George V and Queen Mary in 1935. Given by the artist Sigismund Goetze, the most generous twentieth-century benefactor of the gardens, these gates and those facing Chester Road make imposing and memorable entrances to the gardens. The two kings whose names and arms are most associated with the park, George IV and George V, form a natural sequence, even if their reigns were separated by almost a hundred years.

From a few hundred inhabitants in 1700, its population grew to 5000 in 1740 and to 64,000 by 1801, by which time it had become the richest parish in England. By the middle of the eighteenth century the passage through its streets of cattle, sheep and geese, being driven to Smithfield, had become an increasing nuisance. To resolve the problem, and to provide a fast route for army units, the New Road, one of the first urban bypasses in the world, was constructed. It ran from Paddington, cutting through the south of Marylebone Park, to Pentonville and Islington, then down to the City. First opened in 1756, as little more than a drovers' track, it was soon so much used by private and commercial traffic as to become a major artery. For fifty years after its construction, the New Road and the park's boundaries constituted London's northern limit.

Marylebone Park itself had also become a popular place of excursion for Londoners during the eighteenth century. From a series of maps, those of John Rocque (1746), James Crew (1753) and Thomas Marsh (1789), and from a variety of drawings and paintings, it is possible to get a clear idea of what the park was like during this period. It was almost all given over to grazing. Crew's map shows more than thirty fields, including Butcher's Field, Long Mead and Sedge Field. Although one of the fields was called Sparrowhawk Wood, there were now very few trees other than a small stand in Six Acres Field.

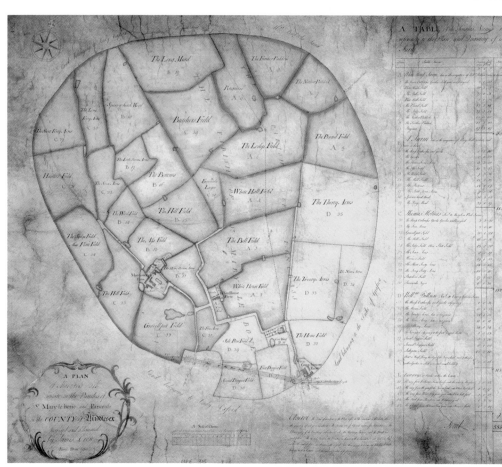

Towards the south of the park were three farms: Marylebone Farm, also known as Daggett's Farm and Willan's Farm, near the site of the present Regent's College; White House Farm, to its east; and Coneyburrow Farm, on the site of Holy Trinity Church, opposite Great Portland Street. Under Thomas Willan, the largest farmer in Middlesex, who farmed over 500 acres in and outside the park, Marylebone Farm expanded to take in White House farmhouse, which became a tea house, the Jew's Harp. A second tea house, the Queen's Head and Artichoke, was established near Coneyburrow Farm. As well as a variety of outbuildings and cottages, there were a number of small businesses near the farms. These included makers of artificial stone, of hair powder and of lacquer for coaches, and a wheelwright's yard. George III's favourite architect, James Wyatt, had his workshop near Coneyburrow Farm. There was also an art gallery built to house the collection of the Austrian Count Truchsess. Two elegant houses stood just north of the New Road, one of them that of John White, surveyor to the Duke of Portland. From Coneyburrow Farm a rough lane went north along the later course of Albany Street, while other tracks and paths ran across the park, including one towards Primrose Hill, already a favourite vantage point.

In the second half of the eighteenth century, the third Duke of Portland, the son of Margaret, Edward Harley's daughter and heir, was the leading landowner in Marylebone. In 1789 he united the main leases of the park, which had previously been divided. He also owned another estate, at Barrow Hill, to the immediate west of Primrose Hill, north of the park and bordering the Eyre Estate in St John's Wood. By this date, the problem of spiritual and bodily provision for the inhabitants of Marylebone had become acute, as there was no adequate parish church and no sufficient burial ground. The duke offered Barrow Hill for the latter, in 1793, in return for permission to drive a diagonal road to it across the park. Had he succeeded, this road would have dictated the future development of the park. His request, however, was turned down on the advice of a man whose influence on the history of Regent's Park was second only to that of John Nash himself.

John Fordyce, Surveyor of Woods and Forests, and Surveyor General of Land Revenues from 1793, was a businesslike Scot intent on improving the efficiency of the Crown Estate. Despite its formal ownership by the monarch, the income from this estate had in fact been exchanged in the eighteenth century for the Civil List, a guaranteed sum agreed by Parliament with new monarchs on their accession. The disposition and use of royal land was therefore now in the hands of the Treasury.

A new style of government efficiency, exemplified by William Pitt the Younger, Tory Prime Minister from 1783 to 1801 and from 1804 to 1806, sought to cut down waste and increase revenue. One of the areas addressed was that of the Crown Estate. A series of reports, the most important ones by Fordyce himself, established that the estates had been slackly administered. These reports set them on a new footing. Marylebone Park was surveyed accurately by George Richardson in 1794, enlarging Crew's earlier map, and the question of its future became the subject of careful consideration.

Fordyce, who realized quite as well as the Duke of Portland the value of Marylebone Park, drew up many of the guidelines for the future Regent's Park. He planned to connect the park to Westminster, by a new road through the West End, to attract the upper classes:

> Distance is best computed by time; and if means could be found to lessen the time of going from Marybone to the Houses of Parliament, the value of the Ground, for building, would be thereby proportionately increased. The best, and probably upon the whole the most advantageous way of doing this, would be by opening a great street from Charing Cross towards a central part of Marybone Park.

He saw the need to offer incentives to development inside a clearly set-out plan, with ornamental water and a canal, together with markets to serve the inhabitants. In 1794 he therefore announced a competition, with a prize of £1000, circulated to all leading architects, for the best plan for developing the park. No submissions were received. It was perhaps found discouraging that there was no provision to reward the work of anyone other than the winner. Moreover, since February 1793, the country had been at war with Revolutionary France, following the execution of Louis XVI.

2

JOHN NASH

LEFT John Nash aged seventy-two, portrait by Sir Thomas Lawrence (1827). Lawrence presents Nash at his most dignified. Nash gave the portrait to Jesus College, Oxford, well known for its Welsh connections.

BELOW LEFT John White's plan, with housing round its perimeter and a lake, almost certainly influenced Nash's own ideas about the park. White, who lived in the park, wished to preserve its rural quality and to allow it to remain a place of recreation open to the public.

BELOW RIGHT Leverton and Chawner's plan. Decidedly inferior to those of White and Nash, Leverton and Chawner's plan contained almost no curves or ornamental features. In their hands, the park would have become little more than an extension of the West End.

War with France continued almost without a break from 1793 to 1815. For most of this time any thoughts of developing Marylebone Park were put to one side. The coming reversion to the crown of the Duke of Portland's leases, in early 1811, however, forced a revival of interest in the park's future. John Fordyce received three plans of development by John White, the Duke of Portland's surveyor, in April 1809. One of these showed a number of the final features of the park, including a lake, a circular road ringed by housing, and open parkland in its north. Fordyce, however, died in July 1809 and it was his successors who revived the £1000 prize in October 1810, with entries required by March 1811. Rather than making it an open competition, they asked the government's own officials to submit proposals.

Of the two submissions received, one was by Thomas Leverton and Thomas Chawner, the surveyors to the Land Revenue Office; the second was by John Nash, the senior architect of the Office of Woods and Forests. Leverton and Chawner's plan was for a standard gridiron extension, in a style similar to that of the existing Portland Estate. Nash's plan, in contrast, had a grand entrance via a circus at the top of Portland Place, leading up from a new street through the West End. Incorporating a canal, running through the centre of the park, and a lake, as well as Outer and Inner Circles, it showed a heavy density of building, with streets, squares and crescents, and twenty-six villas each in substantial grounds. The Inner Circle was a double circus of houses. Such a park would have belonged entirely to those living in it. Nash accompanied his plan with a cogent written report, describing 'the attraction of open space, free air, and the scenery of Nature . . . as allurement and motives for the wealthy part of the Public to establish themselves there', and Arcadian panoramas by A.C. Pugin showing the park and its projected buildings. Nash also offered the prospect of a massive profit for a modest investment, Unsurprisingly, his plan was the one preferred by the commissioners.

John Nash's career before 1811 had been anything but smooth. He was 'a very clever, odd amusing man, with a face like a monkey's but civil and good-humoured to the greatest degree', according to the diarist Mrs Arbuthnot. Even Nash described himself as a 'thick, squat, dwarf

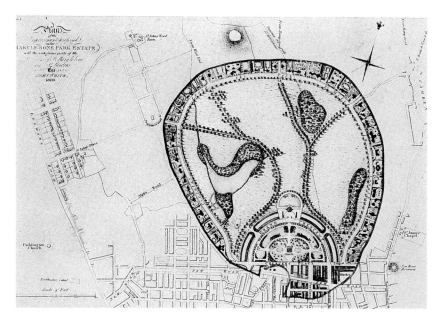

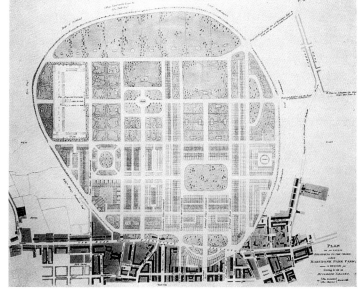

figure, with round head, snub nose and little eyes'. Born in 1752, he had trained as an architect in the office of Sir Robert Taylor and was involved in speculative building, on his own behalf, in Bloomsbury by the age of twenty-five. His first wife, Jane Kerr, was so extravagant that he sent her away from London to Wales. There she had an illegitimate daughter, leading Nash to a failed attempt to divorce her. In 1783 Nash himself went bankrupt. Retreating to Carmarthen, where his family connections and affability made him welcome, he combined a rakish existence with work on small-scale projects.

From this low point he rebuilt his career. Through association with local Whig gentry, he met two major champions of the Picturesque: Sir Uvedale Price, the author of an *Essay on the Picturesque* (1794), who commissioned Nash's highly original triangular Castle House at Aberystwyth; and Richard Payne Knight, whose Downton Castle in Herefordshire was the prototype of Picturesque country houses. Both Price and Knight were Romantics who wished to integrate their houses into the surrounding landscape, rejecting what they saw as the formalism of Capability Brown's regimented parkland.

Nash returned to London and established a country house practice in England, Wales and Ireland, working between 1795 and 1802 with the leading landscape architect of the Picturesque, Humphry Repton. He also began a connection with the Prince Regent, for whom he later rebuilt the Royal Pavilion at Brighton as an oriental pleasure dome between 1815 and 1823. His finances seem to have improved greatly after he married again in 1798. Mary Anne Bradley brought with her seven young cousins named Pennethorne (whose paternity was scandalously linked to the Prince Regent) and considerable wealth of uncertain origin. After the marriage Nash bought two houses in Dover Street and built himself a castle at East Cowes on the Isle of Wight.

Nash's collaboration with Repton on country houses in Picturesque settings was an excellent preparation for his work on Regent's Park. The Picturesque drew on

LEFT Bust of John Nash in the circular portico of his church All Souls, Langham Place (1822–24). The church ingeniously makes a virtue of the change of direction from Regent Street to Portland Place. The bust is a copy by Cecil Thomas, 1956, of the original by William Behnes, 1831.

BELOW LEFT Nash's first, hand-drawn plan, March 1811, shows the interior of the park largely covered by blocks of housing. The canal, connected with a curiously shaped lake, runs through the centre of the park, in which there are two additional stretches of ornamental water. A barracks can be seen in the north of the park.

BELOW RIGHT In Nash's revised plan the barracks still blocks the north of the park. The canal runs nearer the edge. The interior of the park is dotted with villas, including one for the Prince Regent, facing an ornamental body of water.

the idea of illusion and allowed the traditional rules of architecture to be broken. Under the Picturesque it was not considered necessary that the exterior of a house should be consistent in style with its interior. A Gothic exterior could house a modern interior. A classical facade could front offices or a shop. The palaces of Regent's Park, despite their architectural pretensions, were to be terraced housing for the wealthy.

Able to think on a large scale both as an architect and as a developer, Nash was energetic, urbane and ingenious. Neither a learned architect nor a man for detail, he was an indefatigable traveller and a superb salesman – with a great ability to get things started, if not always finished. As with other architects, his work often ran behind schedule and, even more, over budget. Although he had a main assistant, James Morgan, and a large office for an architect of that date, he dealt personally with so many aspects of his work that it is not surprising that it often got out of hand. His career

indeed included an embarrassing number of buildings that fell down or needed to be rebuilt, from an early bridge at Stanford on Teme in Worcestershire to Corsham Court in Wiltshire and, finally, Buckingham Palace.

Nash was appointed to his first official position, as architect to the Office of Woods and Forests, in 1806. This government department, controlled by the Treasury, was responsible for the Crown Estate. As a vision of aristocratic housing, including a clearly argued case for profit to the crown, Nash's first plan for the development of Marylebone Park was an imaginative piece of town planning on the grand scale.

It excluded the public, however, from what had previously been a recreational area. That this would be deeply unpopular, and politically unacceptable at a time of social unrest, was recognized by Spencer Perceval, the Tory Prime Minister and First Lord of the Treasury from 1809. Perceval is mainly remembered today as the only

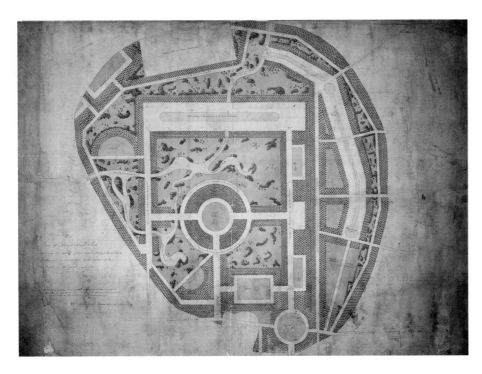

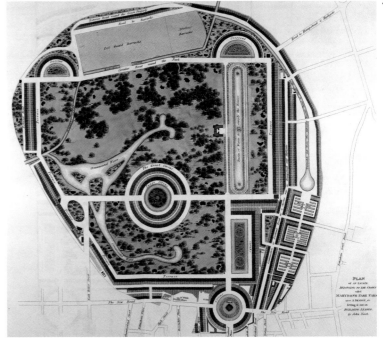

Prime Minister to have been assassinated, shot by John Bellingham in the lobby of the House of Commons in May 1812. Perceval ought, however, also to receive credit for having helped to save Regent's Park from becoming a private enclave. He knew the park well, having often ridden through it on his way to Westminster from his house in Belsize. He had also seen John White's plans, with their generous allocation of open parkland. Perceval summoned Nash to a meeting in Downing Street in August 1811, where he asked him to revise his plan to include 'fewer buildings and a greater extent of open ground'.

Nash, in response, produced a plan pushing back the terraces to the perimeter of the park. Although the Inner Circle remained a double circus, most of the centre of the park was now divided into plots around private villas. While this plan was a move away from the dense urban housing of the first plan, it was not a blueprint for the park as it was actually built. The new plan also drew criticism, of the number of villas, of the position of the canal and of the likely costs, requiring Nash to draw up several further variations over the following years. Its acceptance in outline by the Commissioners of Woods and Forests in October 1811 did, however, bring about the beginning of work on the park, with the roads being made, the lake and the canal (now relegated to the north of the park) dug, and landscaping and tree planting completed between 1811 and 1816.

Both Nash and the commissioners realized that the construction of the park was likely to be a long-term project. The fulfilment of their plans depended on the willingness of wealthy individuals and speculative builders to take up plots on building leases. It was no part of the commissioners' intention to construct the houses in and around the park themselves, as the Treasury's interest as landowner was in improving rents and, ultimately, after ninety-nine years, in getting back whatever was built by the leaseholders. In recognition of the length of time that would be needed, Nash used the strategic planting of trees

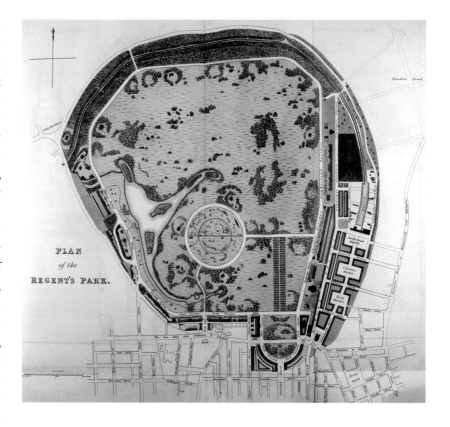

PLAN of the REGENT'S PARK.

as a first step towards development. Hedges would show the sites of the villas and terraces, with slower-growing trees, to hide them from each other in due course, immediately inside the hedges around the villas. This allowed the overall plan to go ahead without a decision being made on the final extent of the building or on the number of villas.

To keep the illusion of grandeur – stone being ruled out by its cost – Nash specified that bricks should be used and covered by stucco: a composite, often oil-based, cement capable of being moulded into ornament and of presenting a fine finish. It could be rusticated to give the appearance of stone and then painted a buff stone colour. The deception proved outstandingly successful, as this glossy uniform finish to the buildings of the park gave them a theatrical impact in keeping with their pretensions.

A later plan by Nash, engraved in 1826, shows many features of the park that are familiar today. The canal now runs inside the northern perimeter of the park, the entrance to the park is no longer a circus and a few real, rather than proposed, villas are visible. The barracks has moved to Albany Street.

In the early years of the park, little was built. One disaster followed another. While almost no progress was made on either the terraces or the villas, the cost of the canal planned to run through the north of the park far exceeded its budget, a problem compounded when the canal company's secretary, Thomas Homer, absconded with company funds in 1815. The spoil from the lake and canal, spread over the park, caused problems with building stability, and the early tree plantation failed because of waterlogged soil.

This slow beginning was followed by intense activity in the eight years after 1818, which saw nearly all of the initial construction of the park. Nash also completed Regent Street between 1813 and 1826. Full of architectural variety, it ran from St James's Park and Carlton House Terrace, via Waterloo Place, Piccadilly and Oxford Circus, to join up with Portland Place next to Nash's new church of All Souls, Langham Place, a striking pivot for his new route.

The profitability of the park, however, proved to be far lower than Nash had projected; and its costs, and those of Regent Street, greatly exceeded his original estimates. Even worse, the costs on Buckingham Palace, which between 1825 and 1830 was being rebuilt to Nash's designs, ran completely out of control. In 1826, following an economic downturn, the Treasury decided to bring work in the park to an end. Although the true reason was Nash's inability to control costs, the commissioners' justification was that:

> the original Plans for occupying so much of the Ground, and particularly in the interior of the Park, by Building, would so far destroy the scenery, and shut out so many beautiful views towards the Villages of Highgate and Hampstead, as to render it very advisable to reduce the number of Sites to be appropriated for Villas, and also to leave open the Northern Boundary of the Estate, formerly intended to be built upon.

In reality, the plan for the park changed many times during its construction and development, with no consensus as to how much would be filled with building in the end. The Treasury's decision meant that only the south of the park was left with anything like the Picturesque ensemble planned by Nash. The north of the park, the terraces around its perimeter now abandoned, remained without structure other than the canal cutting, a vacuum partly filled by the opening of the Zoo in 1828.

In 1830, after criticism of his work on Buckingham Palace, and its cost, became impossible to ignore, Nash was dismissed; although an enquiry acquitted him of dishonesty. He retired to his castle on the Isle of White, where he died in 1835. Whatever his shortcomings – and very few of his individual buildings can be described as unqualified masterpieces – there is no doubt that he had a greater influence on London than any other architect, including Wren. It was his energy and commitment that drove through Regent Street, still the principal link between Westminster and Regent's Park. He redrew the whole area around St James's Park, including Buckingham Palace, Carlton House Terrace and Trafalgar Square. His most lasting and typical achievement, however, was and is Regent's Park. According to the writer Henry Crabb Robinson:

> I really think that this enclosure, with the new street leading to it from Carlton House, will give a sort of glory to the Regent's government, which will be more felt by remote posterity than the victories of Trafalgar and Waterloo, glorious as they are.

3

TERRACES

The most striking feature of Regent's Park is undoubtedly its terraces, which run almost continuously from Gloucester Gate around the south of the park to Hanover Gate. The terraces are spectacular exercises in illusion. While looking like palaces, they were in reality built as individual houses for the wealthy. Terraced housing was a British speciality, unknown in continental Europe but a prime component in the building of Georgian and Victorian cities. As well as making up many London squares, this form of housing ranged from the grand stone terraces, circuses and crescents of Bath and Edinburgh to modest suburban developments in brick. Nash's stuccoed Regent's Park terraces, and Carlton House Terrace overlooking St James's Park, are the supreme examples of the domestic terrace at its most artificial and grandiose.

Nash's original plan showed two circuses in the Inner Circle, to be called Prince of Wales Circus and Princess Charlotte's Circus, and other terraces in the interior of the park. Carrick and Munster Terraces were intended for the north of the park, while Renfrew and Rothesay Terraces also appear on one of his early plans. His main revised plan showed terraces surrounding the whole of the park, except where the government proposed to build a barracks on its northern boundary. When the barracks was moved to Albany Street, this made space for the Zoo.

All the terraces, built and unbuilt, were given names reflecting titles held by the Prince Regent and his siblings, adding to the cachet of royal patronage already lent by the name of 'The Regent's Park' itself, formally adopted in 1813. The Prince himself, as Duke of Cornwall and Earl of Chester, gave his name to Cornwall Terrace, Chester Terrace and Chester Road. Of his brothers, Adolphus was Duke of Cambridge; Augustus was Duke of Sussex; Edward (the father of Queen Victoria) was Duke of Kent and Strathearn; Ernest was Duke of Cumberland and King of Hanover; Frederick was Duke of York and Albany; and William (who succeeded his brother as William IV in 1830) was Duke of Clarence and St Andrews. Their sister, Mary, was married to William, Duke of Gloucester, who was also Earl of Ulster. None of the royal dukes had more than this nominal connection with the park.

Of course, Nash could not build the park alone: he was dependent on wealthy clients or builders coming forward to take leases. The building of the terraces was a slow process, with few offers made to take up building leases in the early years. The first terrace to be built, Park Crescent at the top of Portland Place, begun in 1812 by the speculative builder Charles Mayor, was a disaster, with Mayor going bankrupt in 1816. This led to an alteration in the plan.

LEFT The grandest of all Nash terraces was not one of those in Regent's Park but Carlton House Terrace in St James's Park (1827–33), a backdrop to the Mall, the ceremonial route leading to Buckingham Palace. Nash completely remodelled St James's Park, replacing its existing central canal with the lake familiar today. St James's Park and Regent's Park were linked by Nash's Regent Street.

RIGHT Clarence Terrace and Sussex Place seen across the lake.

Cumberland Terrace (1826) is the most imposing of all the terraces in Regent's Park, in keeping with Nash's intention that it should face a villa designed for the Prince Regent. Its three main blocks, with Ionic columns, are separated by two grand arches leading into courtyards. The central block has a pavilion surmounted by a pediment. The statues in the pediment, where Britannia is shown with the arts, sciences and trades of her empire, are by J.G. Bubb. Additional loosely classical figures, also by Bubb, are to be seen at other points on the terrace. Unimpressive at close quarters, they are striking when seen at a distance. All the original statues were repaired or replaced after the Second World War. The upkeep of the terraces is in the hands of a statutory body, the Crown Estate Paving Commission, whose initials can be seen above the name of the terrace. Behind all the terraces are mews for stabling. To the north of the terrace is St Katharine's Precinct.

Hanover Terrace (1822), the best preserved of the terraces and the most correct in architectural terms, has three porticoes carried on a ground-floor arcade. Giant Doric columns support pediments with classical figures, mostly female, by an unknown sculptor. The terrace has been the home of many literary and musical figures, including H.G. Wells and Ralph Vaughan Williams.

Susssex Place (1822–23). Three flat and two curved ranges, with Corinthian columns standing on an arcade, topped with pointed hexagonal domes. No longer divided into individual houses, and rebuilt retaining the original facade after serious damage in the Second World War, Sussex Place now houses the London School of Business Studies.

Clarence Terrace (1823), a shorter terrace with a single Corinthian portico. Originally the wings were supposed to be joined to the centre by screens of Ionic columns. To increase the profitabiity of the terrace, James Burton added houses immediately behind the screens. The whole terrace has been rebuilt, behind a facsimile facade.

Cornwall Terrace (1821), the first terrace in the park to be built. Designed by Decimus Burton, it is Corinthian, with a central portico with free-standing giant columns. The end facing Clarence Gate has a bow window with four caryatids. The tower of the Abbey National building can be seen behind the terrace.

No. 15 Gloucester Gate, one of Nash's minor villas, its Ionic columns facing originally towards the Cumberland Market branch of the Regent's Canal, now filled in. The Doric columns and cast-iron gates of the original entrance to the park here were removed when the road was widened in 1878. The lodges which stood on either side of the gate now stand together on its north side.

At the entrance to the park, instead of a circus, two terraces were to face each other across Park Square.

The more favourable economic climate of the 1820s, however, meant that all the terraces were built or on the stocks by 1826. James Burton, who had already developed much of Bloomsbury, was to prove the most active builder in the park. Although their relations were often strained, Nash relied heavily on Burton's ability to mobilize a large and skilled workforce. James Burton's son Decimus Burton became the second architect of the park, the designer of terraces, villas and the Colosseum, as well as the Zoo and the Royal Botanic Gardens.

The terraces were erected under the general supervision of Nash, who approved the plans submitted to him by the builders and their architects. He himself designed Cumberland Terrace, Hanover Terrace and Sussex Place, and provided facade designs for Park Square and York Terrace. Decimus Burton designed Clarence and Cornwall Terraces. The limit to the control exercised by Nash is, however, exemplified by Gloucester Terrace, where the architect, John Joseph Scoles, made the details twice the intended size without Nash's noticing. James Burton erected Chester, Clarence and Cornwall Terraces, and shared York Terrace with William Mountford Nurse, the builder of Cumberland and Ulster Terraces and of Park Square West. Richard Mott built Cambridge Terrace, Chester Gate and Gloucester Terrace, and John Mackell Adams built Hanover Terrace.

Exact finishing dates are hard to give, as the houses in the terraces underwent extensive internal fitting and decoration by their new occupants. Park Crescent,

LEFT Chester Terrace (1825). Over 900 feet long and divided into nine parts, the terrace has three porticoes with projecting Corinthian columns. At either end triumphal arches link the terrace to additional houses which the builder, James Burton, put in against Nash's wishes. It was originally surmounted by sculpted figures by J.G. Bubb, but these were taken down at Nash's insistence. Some of the displaced figures almost certainly found a new home on Cumberland Terrace.

LEFT Cambridge Terrace (1825). Plainly built, with rusticated columns at the centre and ends of the ground floor, and heavily restored.

BELOW Chester Gate (1825), between Chester Terrace and Cambridge Terrace, leading from the park to Nash's service area in and behind Albany Street. A garden, originally flanking the entry from the Cambridge Terrace side, has been lost to road widening.

LEFT AND ABOVE York Terrace East (1822). Nash separated the two halves of York Terrace – originally intended as a single terrace – to take advantage of the vista provided by Thomas Hardwick's new parish church of St Marylebone. A short additional range, nominally part of York Terrace but with Corinthinian pillars, lies to the east of York Terrace East. The two ranges are spearated by Doric Villa, two semi-detached houses disguised as a Doric temple.

BELOW York Terrace West (1822). Both halves of York Terrace have Doric colonnades on the ground storey broken by Ionic pavilions. The entrances to the houses are at the back, with communal gardens in front.

however, was finished in 1821, as was Cornwall Terrace. Hanover and York Terraces followed in 1822; Clarence Terrace, Park Square East and Sussex Place in 1823; Park Square West, Ulster Place and Ulster Terrace in 1824; and Albany, Cambridge and Chester Terraces in 1825. Finally, Cumberland Place, Cumberland Terrace and St Andrews Place were built by 1826; and Gloucester and Kent Terraces by 1827. Kent Terrace, facing outwards from the park, remains an anomaly.

York Terrace, originally planned as a single long range, was divided in two by Nash to allow another entrance to the park. Marylebone had finally decided where to site their new parish church, designed by Thomas Hardwick and built in 1817 at a cost of £60,000. York Gate (1822) used the magnificent new church as its focus to great effect, with the two wings of York Terrace running to either side along the park. The long-term problem of where to bury the parishioners of Marylebone had been solved in 1814 by the building of a chapel, also by Thomas Hardwick, at St John's Wood and the establishment of a burial ground there.

The terraces (all much criticized by purists for being incorrect in academic terms) have enough variety in their

RIGHT Ulster Terrace (1824), with Ionic columns on the ground storey and two sets of bow windows. Now converted into offices, the terrace echoes St Andrews Place on the opposite side of Park Square.

BELOW Park Square West (1823–24), originally intended to be built as the curved northern part of a circus completing Park Crescent, looks across a communal garden, connected to the garden of Park Crescent by a tunnel under the Marylebone Road. It has Ionic columns on the ground floor on either side of a rusticated central section. Above both runs an arcade of round-headed windows. Its return front on the park end is formed by Ulster Terrace.

BELOW Park Square East, matching Park Square West. Its central range, which housed the Diorama, an early version of the cinema brought to London by Louis Daguerre, the inventor of the daguerreotype, was the first section of the terrace to be built.

use of architectural orders and other details to give them each an individual flavour. Some are relatively modest in length; others, such as Cumberland, Chester and York Terraces, are of enormous size. There are also smaller blocks and individual houses, such as Cumberland Place and the Doric Villa, and lodges to provide variety. Chester Place is

set back behind its grander namesake. Chester, Cumberland, Gloucester and Hanover Terraces all have pediments adorned with sculptured groups. Chester Terrace has two triumphal entry arches placed at right angles to the main facade. Each terrace has its classical references, ranging from the simple Ionic columns of Ulster Terrace to the

BELOW LEFT Gloucester Lodge (1826), once known as Strathearn Lodge, was built for Sir Brooke Taylor, the brother of the Master of St Katharine's Hospital. The northern end of Gloucester Terrace is behind.

BELOW RIGHT Gloucester Terrace (1827), also sometimes called Gloucester Gate, with Ionic columns and three porches, only the end ones with pediments.

massive Corinthian pillars of Chester Terrace. Cornwall Terrace has caryatids facing Clarence Gate, an entrance only from 1823. Sussex Place has hexagonal domes which were much derided when first built.

Although many men and women of note lived in the terraces, and the occasional grandee in the villas, Regent's Park never replaced Hyde Park as the home or meeting place of the fashionable. While the terraces looked magnificent, their shining stucco hides the fact that they were built on clay with minimal foundations and without damp courses. This is one reason why it was never easy to lease them out and which led to their slow decline in the years before 1939, by which time the park had become distinctly unfashionable. Blackened by soot and sometimes untenanted, they decayed as their stucco peeled.

During the Second World War, when much of the park was given over to the military, the terraces suffered bomb damage. The lack of funds for maintenance caused further deterioration. This left them in such a dilapidated state by the end of war that it was even suggested that they should be pulled down. There was 'not a single terrace, with the partial exception of Hanover Terrace . . . which does not give the impression of hopeless destruction'. Marylebone Council was keen to replace them with affordable housing, while the Royal Institute of British Architects recommended partial replacement with new buildings. The Gorrell Commission, which reported in 1947 on their pitiful condition, recommended their restoration, a conclusion accepted in Cabinet on the casting vote of the Prime Minister, Clement Attlee. Their fate still hung in

BELOW Chester Place (1825–26). Set behind Cumberland Place and Chester Terrace, and little known to most visitors to the park, Chester Place is simply designed with Tuscan pilasters.

BOTTOM Kent Terrace (1827). The only major terrace facing away from the park, Kent Terrace, in Park Road, once had Sussex Lodge to its south and Albany and Abbey Villas to its north. It also originally looked out at the early villas of St John's Wood, swept away in the 1890s by the building of the Great Central Railway.

the balance until 1957, when the Crown Commissioners allocated up to ten million pounds to restoration.

Since then, all of the terraces have been restored by the Crown Estate, with many of the houses converted and leased as offices. Where possible, the terraces have simply been restored, as with Hanover and Kent Terraces; but where there was severe bomb damage more drastic measures were taken. Park Crescent, Clarence Terrace and part of York Terrace have been completely rebuilt with facsimile facades. Sussex Place has been rebuilt behind its original facade. Other terraces have been partly rebuilt and partly restored.

In the line of Nash terraces, five buildings stand out as extraneous. South of Gloucester Terrace, St Katharine's Hospital was designed by Ambrose Poynter, a disaffected ex-pupil of Nash, in Neo-Gothic style – to Nash's intense annoyance. It was built in brick but without stucco (though faced in stone towards the park) to rehouse the St Katharine's Hospital, founded originally by Queen Matilda, the wife of King Stephen, in 1148. With land given directly to the hospital by the Crown Estate, this moved to Regent's Park from east of the Tower of London in 1825, to make way for St Katharine's Docks. Since 1950 it has housed the Danish Church in London.

To the south of Cambridge Terrace is Cambridge Gate, built in a French style in 1876–80. Unlike any of Nash's terraces, it is faced with Bath stone. It replaced Decimus Burton's Colosseum, a sixteen-sided building, with a diameter of 130 feet, a dome larger than that of St Paul's and a fine portico. Drawing comparisons with and inspiration from the Pantheon in Rome, it was erected, between 1824 and 1827, to display a panorama of London drawn by the artist E.T. Parris from a cabin on the top of St Paul's Cathedral while the latter's dome was being repaired. With its 40,000 square feet of canvas, the scheme was ambitious. This, and the slow completion of the project, brought about the bankruptcy of its originator, Thomas Horner.

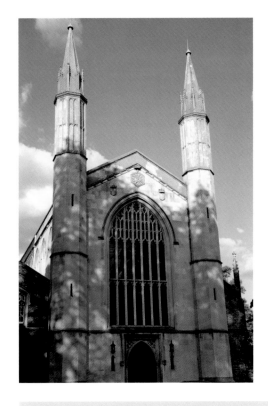

St Katharine's Precinct, by Ambrose Poynter (1825–27). St Katharine's Hospital, originally next to the Tower of London, was dedicated to the spiritual rather than the physical health of those to whom it ministered. Its new church, echoing King's College Chapel, Cambridge, and containing the heraldic arms of the queens of England, is flanked by housing for the brothers and sisters of the hospital. On the wings facing the park are arms commemorating the hospital's foundation by Queen Matilda in 1148, its refoundation by Queen Eleanor of Provence in 1273 (shown left) and its restoration by George IV in 1828. The hospital's medieval and later fittings, which were brought to the park in the 1820s, were moved after the Second World War to the Royal Foundation of St Katharine in Limehouse. The magnificent tomb of the Duke of Exeter, Henry V's uncle and a hero of Agincourt, has been moved to the chapel of St Peter ad Vincula in the Tower of London, where the duke is buried with his first and third wives. St Katharine's Church has been the Danish Church in London since 1950.

York Gate (1821–22), the grandest entrance to the park, with Ionic facades on either side of St Mary's Church. During the development of the park, the parish of St Marylebone finally came to a decision about where to build its new parish church by Thomas Hardwick (1813–17). With a six-columned Corinthian portico, its circular tower has golden angels, by John Rossi, around its cupola. Nash adjusted his original plan for York Terrace, splitting it into two ranges, to allow an entrance from the south of the park focused on the new church.

BELOW Decimus Burton's Colosseum (1824–27), seen from York Bridge in a steel engraving by T.H. Shepherd (1827). The Colosseum had a magnificent Doric portico with six columns. The gardens around it were 'laid out so as to appear much more extensive than they really are and comprise conservatories, waterfalls, fountains, a Swiss cottage, a marine cave and grotto, all of beautiful construction'. In the foreground of the engraving, a water spaniel is in hopeful pursuit of ducks.

OPPOSITE, ABOVE The Royal College of Physicians (1961–64) by Sir Denys Lasdun, with its principal elevation facing away from the park.

OPPOSITE, BELOW Slit windows, irregularly placed, look out over the college's blue brick lecture theatre and on to St Andrews Place (1823–26), a terrace with Ionic columns echoing Ulster Terrace but with a mansion, with a Corinthian portico, at its eastern end.

Despite the added attractions of a lift to the top of the building for views over London, the display of the original ball and cross from St Paul's, and fine gardens around it, the Colosseum never proved profitable. This remained the case even when it was turned into a concert hall. After years of closure and decay, it was pulled down in 1875.

Next to Cambridge Place is Sir Denys Lasdun's Royal College of Physicians (1961-64), of concrete covered with off-white mosaic tiles but flanked by a lecture theatre of blue engineering brick. It stands on the site of Someries House, an orphan asylum for the daughters of clergymen and officers, designed without charge by Nash but damaged in the Second World War. The college is often criticized as being out of place in Regent's Park, and indeed Lasdun deliberately faced it away from the park; but its bold angles, fine materials and strength of design, with its main raised rectangle seemingly floating without adequate support, makes it a distinguished piece of modern architecture with a positive presence. This cannot be claimed for the Royal College of Obstetricians and Gynaecologists, by Louis de Soissons (1960), north of Hanover Terrace but set back from the Outer Circle. It replaced Sussex Lodge, a villa possibly designed by Nash himself but demolished in 1938.

Finally, the copper dome of the London Central Mosque draws attention to itself across the western part of the park. From 1946 the Islamic Cultural Centre had been based in Albany Cottage (an early villa also known as North Villa), which led to its becoming the site, in a changing world, of the present mosque. Designed by Sir Frederick Gibberd in 1972, the dome of the mosque can claim to be an echo of Nash's Royal Pavilion in Brighton, but the interior is plain, with its main hall, designed for 1800 worshippers, square and functional. In exchange for the Crown Estate's permission to demolish the villa and to build in the park, the Church of England was given land for a new church in Cairo.

The perimeter of the northern half of the park, where there are no nineteenth-century terraces, is very different from that of the south. The Zoo, another Regent's Park anomaly, occupies the boundary, reinforced by the Regent's Canal, between the main park and Primrose Hill. Between St John's Wood and the Zoo, a strip of parkland makes up the north bank of the canal, overlooked by modern flats outside the Crown Estate. On the Outer Circle to the west of the Zoo are intrusive reproduction villas by Quinlan Terry. East of the Zoo, a car park has replaced a redundant stretch of canal. Here the park is overlooked by a series of small villas on Prince Albert Road, built in the 1840s.

Besides the main park, with its grand buildings, all Nash's plans included a service area for the villas and terraces. He insisted on the building of a branch of the Regent's Canal running down the east of the park, and under a bridge at Gloucester Gate, to Cumberland Basin. Here he intended to establish three markets: Cumberland Market for hay, replacing the Haymarket in St James's; Clarence Market for vegetables; and York Market for meat. In the event, only Cumberland Market was built. Clarence Market became a nursery garden with some housing; and York Market turned into the unpretentious but attractive housing of Munster Square.

Running north to south, parallel with the eastern length of the Outer Circle on the line of an earlier farm track, Albany Street separated the terraces of the park from the service area. The only public entry from Albany Street into the main body of the park was at Chester Gate, in keeping with Nash's determination to shield the park from the less prestigious neighbourhoods, and their inhabitants, around it. Albany Street was also the final home of the Life Guards barracks originally planned for the north of the park and built by Nash in a very plain style.

Albany Street itself was once much more attractive than it is today, with plain but handsome terraces, some of them the reverse of terraces in the main park, as well as an ophthalmic hospital and a riding school. In 1837 Nash's architectural heir, James Pennethorne, designed

Christ Church, Albany Street. Its interior was subsequently reworked by William Butterfield, with glass by Dante Gabriel Rossetti. A later church, St Mary Magdalene in Longford Street, was aimed at working-class worshippers. As well as the rebuilt Queen's Head and Artichoke, relocated from the main park, there were numerous other pubs, including the only pub designed by Nash himself, the York and Albany, at the top of Park Village East.

Little remains of what Albany Street once was, other than the barracks, a few original houses and Christ Church. Whatever the merits of Denys Lasdun's Royal College, its Albany Street front is a brutal replacement of the terrace previously there. From the 1930s the wharves around the canal basin began to be replaced by blocks of flats. The branch of the canal leading to Cumberland Basin was sold back to the Crown Estate in 1938 and, being of no commercial value but acting as a targeting aid to German bombers, was filled in in 1942 and 1943. The area was, nevertheless, heavily bombed in the Second World War. In 1971, the Crown Commissioners sold much of the area to St Pancras Borough Council, which redeveloped it with poorly planned and unattractive housing blocks. On the site of the basin itself, protected by Act of Parliament from being built on, there are now allotments.

LEFT The London Central Mosque (1972–78), by Sir Frederick Gibberd and Partners, stands on the site of Albany Cottage, described by Elmes in *Metropolitan Improvements* (1827–28): 'As a specimen of the English cottage ornée, it is scarcely to be surpassed.' The mosque, together with its offices and residential block, is deliberately functional, with few architectural or other ornamental features.

RIGHT Nash's plan for a vegetable market in Clarence Market, as part of the service area of the park, was doomed to failure. Vegetables, however, are now grown privately on the site of the centrepiece of his plans for the area, Cumberland Basin, the terminus of a specially built branch of the Regent's Canal.

4

VILLAS

As substantial houses for the wealthy and well-connected, villas proclaimed the exclusivity of a development far more effectively than terraces. It is not surprising that all Nash's plans for Regent's Park included villas, each surrounded by its own land. The initial layout of the park showed where each villa would be, 'so planted that no villa should see any other, but each should appear to possess the whole of the Park; and that the streets of Houses which overlook the Park should not see the Villas'. The aim, echoing Picturesque ideas, was the creation of an illusion of privacy in a country setting.

In keeping with the name of the park, the grandest of the villas was to have been that of the Prince Regent himself. Described as a 'guinguette', a place of entertainment outside normal licensing controls, it was sited to the west of what later became the Broad Walk facing Cumberland Terrace, appropriately the grandest of the terraces, with an ornamental canal between the two. The Broad Walk was to have been the avenue leading to it. The Duke of Wellington, the hero of Waterloo, was also offered the Inner Circle as the site for a magnificent villa.

No detailed plans were ever drawn up for the guinguette. The Prince Regent, from 1820 King George IV, preoccupied with Nash's rebuilding of Buckingham Palace and with the Royal Pavilion in Brighton, showed little interest in the park named after him. The villa never became more substantial than the planting that marked its site. The Duke of Wellington also refused the offer made to him, preferring Apsley House in Hyde Park.

Although there had been many enquiries before the park was laid out, very few men with the necessary means to build a villa came forward during the early years of the park. Only three of the villa sites had been let by 1817, one of them to Nash's chief builder, James Burton. Because of this, and because of later official limitation, the projected number of villas fell from over fifty at one point to no more than eight. In the end, six villas were built in the central area of the park (Hertford

House, Holford House, the Holme, St John's Lodge, St Katharine's Lodge and South Villa), with Grove House on the north bank of the Regent's Canal. To these should be added six villas on the park periphery (Albany Cottage; Abbey, Gloucester, Hanover and Sussex Lodges; and Doric Villa). Because those who commissioned the villas were men of wealth and status, who usually employed their own architects, Nash had little control over what was built, even where he had approved the plans. In some cases, such as St Katharine's Lodge, he had no control at all.

The first three villas were built on the Inner Circle. The Holme, designed for James Burton by his son Decimus, was built by 1818. Overlooking the lake, the Holme was initially criticized by the commissioners as unworthy of its position. Even Nash admitted that 'it is to be lamented, for the beauty of the Park, that Mr Burton was *allowed* to build the sort of house he has built.' The reasons for the commissioners' strictures are unclear. The villa, if not pretentious, was elegant and well proportioned, with Ionic pilasters and a small dome. The Holme was enlarged by the addition of a ballroom in 1911 and then remodelled by Paul Phipps, a pupil of Lutyens and father of the entertainer and impressionist Joyce Grenfell, in the late 1930s.

On the north-east of the Inner Circle, John Raffield designed St John's Lodge, built by 1819 for Charles Augustus Tulk. Tulk was soon replaced as tenant by the Marquess Wellesley, the elder brother of the Duke of Wellington, who commissioned Decimus Burton to enlarge the villa, and then by Isaac Goldschmid, Baron Palmeira, a leading campaigner in the struggle to remove Jewish legal disabilities. Goldschmid engaged Sir Charles Barry, the architect of the Houses of Parliament, to make a further enlargement.

Raffield's villa was of two storeys, its prominent porch with Doric pillars topped by two Coade stone lions by the sculptor John Flaxman. With lower wings on each side, the centre had a four-light window with Corinthian

The Holme. Standing in a superb position, the Holme was built for and by John Nash's principal builder and supporter, James Burton, and occupied by him and his family between 1818 and 1831. It was designed by Burton's tenth child, Decimus, as one of his earliest works. Decimus went on to design many other buildings in the park, as well as the Athenaeum, Hyde Park Corner and the Palm House at Kew. The Holme's interior and exterior have been greatly altered since it was first built, with Corinthian columns replacing the original Ionic ones. The villa has a garden designed by the landscape architect Sir Geoffrey Jellicoe.

St John's Lodge, steel engraving by T.H. Shepherd. The original St John's Lodge, built and occupied by 1819, was considerably more modest than its present-day successor, which is easily the most imposing of the surviving villas in the park, even though now set in greatly reduced grounds. In the later nineteenth century, it was the London home of the eccentric third Marquess of Bute, reputedly the richest man in the world, and a patron of architecture and interior decoration on an heroic scale.

South Villa (1816–17), with its Ionic portico, steel engraving by T.H. Shepherd. Today only the lodge of South Villa, on York Bridge, survives. When Bedford College (founded in Bedford Square by Elizabeth Jesser Reid in 1849) outgrew its original accommodation, it acquired the lease of the villa in 1908. While the villa itself survived, in changed form, until 1930, its grounds were used for a major expansion of the college. When Bedford College moved to Egham, in 1985, the buildings and surrounding grounds were taken over by Regent's College.

columns above the porch. Between 1846 and 1847 Barry added a third storey, and brought forward the two wings, between which he introduced a new entrance hall with a pedimented porch. In keeping with this Italianizing of the Greek original, a new ballroom was decorated by Ambrose Poynter, who drew his inspiration from Raphael. In 1889 the villa was acquired by the third Marquess of Bute, whose fabulous wealth was drawn from the development of Cardiff Docks to ship Welsh coal. Although the marquess died in 1900, his widow lived on there until 1916. From 1937 to 1958, St John's was the University of London Institute of Archaeology, under the flamboyant Sir Mortimer Wheeler.

The first villa to be built, however, was South Villa in 1816-17, probably designed by the precocious Decimus Burton. Its most noteworthy tenant was the astronomer George Bishop, who had an observatory in its grounds. Rebuilt in terracotta between 1879 and 1883, it was taken over by Bedford College, a university college for women, in 1908. This was not the first attempt by an academic institution to establish itself in the park. In 1828, when the newly founded King's College asked for the use of the land inside the Inner Circle, its request was rejected on the grounds that one zoo was enough for the park.

In 1823 Decimus Burton designed Grove House, on the north bank of the Regent's Canal opposite St John's Wood Chapel. Commissioned by the scientist George Bellas Greenough, it had an imposing Ionic portico and a circular salon topped by a dome. Grove House has preserved much of its original form. From 1909 until

Grove House, steel engraving by T.H. Shepherd. On the banks of the Regent's Canal, Grove House was designed by Decimus Burton and built by his father, James Burton, by 1823. Its most notable twentieth-century owner, Sigismund Goetze, was prolific in his gifts to the park. He also gave the striking bronze war memorial, of St George and the Dragon, facing St John's Wood Church. Until recently the headquarters of the Nuffield Foundation, Grove House is now privately occupied.

1939 it was the home of the artist Sigismund Goetze, a generous benefactor of the park, who converted the stables into a studio and decorated the drawing room with scenes from Ovid's *Metamorphoses*.

Burton also designed Hertford House for the third Marquess of Hertford in 1825. Nicknamed the Caliph of Regent's Park, and an art collector with a penchant for amorous French paintings, Hertford is considered the original for the Marquess of Steyne, Thackeray's libertine in *Vanity Fair*, and for the Marquess of Monmouth in Disraeli's *Coningsby*. He renamed his villa St Dunstan's, after acquiring the clock from the rebuilt church of St Dunstan's-in-the-West in Fleet Street and installing it in a campanile. The villa's use as a hostel for those blinded in the First World War led to its name being given to a principal charity for the blind. After the First World War St Dunstan's also occupied St John's Lodge.

Hanover Lodge, facing St Dunstan's Villa across the Outer Circle, was designed by Decimus Burton and built for Sir Robert Arbuthnot, a hero of the Peninsular War, by 1827. Unpretentious in style, with four Ionic columns facing its garden, it was later leased to the flamboyant naval adventurer, Sir Thomas Cochrane, and from 1911 to another, Lord Beatty, the hero of Jutland, for whom the interior was remodelled by Sir Edwin Lutyens.

St Katharine's Lodge, a Neo-Gothic villa out of keeping with the others in the park, was built by Ambrose Poynter for General Sir Herbert Taylor, Master of St Katharine's Hospital, between the Outer Circle and the Broad Walk in 1827. Sir Herbert, a confidant of Queen Charlotte, George IV and William IV, was instrumental in the move of St Katharine's from the Tower to Regent's Park, a move eased by providing him with a villa near the new site of the hospital.

The last major nineteenth-century house to be built in the park, begun in 1833, was also the largest. Holford House, in the north-west of the park, was designed by Decimus Burton and included a giant portico at its

Hertford House, steel engraving by T.H. Shepherd. The one undoubted grandee to build a villa in Regent's Park in its early years, the third Marquess of Hertford used Hertford House, which he renamed St Dunstan's Villa, for entertainment. It housed some of his remarkable collection of art, which formed a major part of what later became the Wallace Collection. Designed by Decimus Burton and set in substantial private grounds, the villa was in use by 1829. It was demolished in 1936.

St Katharine's Lodge, steel engraving by T.H. Shepherd. Set in grounds inside the park opposite St Katharine's Hospital, St Katharine's Lodge was built by 1827 and occupied by the master of the hospital, General Sir Herbert Taylor, an adroit courtier whose influence with George IV and William IV was of great use to the government. Turned into a hospital in the First World War, it was badly damaged by a flying bomb in 1944 and subsequently pulled down. Its site can be discerned in the unevenness of the ground on St Katharine's Green.

centre flanked by pavilions with cupolas at each end. James Holford, a bachelor wine merchant, lived there in state until his death on 1854, after which an auction of the contents took fourteen days to complete. It was subsequently occupied by Regent's Park Baptist College.

Over the years since they were built, and mirroring the history of the terraces, many of the villas have undergone substantial alteration. St Dunstan's, the renamed Hertford Villa, was acquired in 1936 by the American heiress Barbara Hutton. (She was later married briefly to Cary Grant, when they were unkindly known as 'Cash and Cary'.) She demolished the villa, which was run down, having been left uninhabited and then damaged by fire, and commissioned a new one, designed by Leonard Rome Guthrie of the architects Wimperis and Simpson, in a neo-Georgian style that would not have been out of place in Virginia. In the face of Crown Estate objections, she successfully insisted on the use of red brick. The new house took its name, Winfield House, from Barbara

Hutton's grandfather, Frank Winfield Woolworth, the founder of the chain store. After the Second World War, during which the house was used by the Royal Air Force, she wrote to President Truman offering it as a gift to the American people. Since 1954 it has been the home of the American Ambassadors to the Court of St James.

Although it is used to entertain thousands of Americans and other guests every year, and as a base for visiting American Presidents, the restriction on casual entry is clearly signalled by the armed policemen on guard outside the house. The thick hedge and fencing, screening its boundary, make the house and its garden invisible from the park – except from the minaret of the Mosque.

Several other villas have totally disappeared. St Katharine's Lodge – used as a hospital in and after the First World War – and Holford House were bombed in the Second World War and subsequently demolished. On the Inner Circle, Bedford College added a new building by Basil Champneys in 1913 while retaining South Villa.

Hanover Lodge, steel engraving by T.H. Shepherd. Designed by Decimus Burton and occupied from 1827, Hanover Lodge was one of a number of lesser villas outside the Outer Circle. Among a series of remarkable owners and inhabitants, Joseph Bonaparte, Napoleon's elder brother and once the King of Spain, lived here for some months in 1840.

Holford House, begun in 1833; view taken from auction catalogue, 1854. The last of the nineteenth-century villas to be built in the park, Holford House was also the largest and most expensive. Designed by Decimus Burton for the wine merchant James Holford, it was set in extensive grounds. Following Holford's death, it became Regent's Park Baptist College between 1854 and the Second World War, during which it was badly bombed. It was subsequently demolished, but traces of its site remain in the north-west of the park.

Then in 1930, despite many protests, it demolished the villa to replace it with undistinguished work by Maxwell Ayrton. Badly bombed in the Second World War, when it housed the Dutch Government in Exile, and very short of teaching space and accommodation, the college acquired the leases of a number of the park villas.

St John's Lodge and the Holme provided highly congenial locations for departments of Bedford College, as did Hanover Lodge, which was acquired by Bedford College in 1948. Lutyens's work in Hanover Lodge was swept away in the early 1960s when the villa became part of a hall of residence. In the 1980s the main block of the hall of residence was in turn demolished, the site and strip of the park along the canal being filled with neo-classical villas by the architect Quinlan Terry. Bedford College amalgamated with Royal Holloway College in 1985 and moved to Egham. Since then its buildings have been used by Regent's College.

Hanover Lodge itself has now been rebuilt as a private villa in a much-changed form, greatly larger than the original, with little that is older preserved. St John's Lodge, one of the most desirable residences in London, has until recently been occupied by the profligate Prince Jefri, brother of the Sultan of Brunei. Grove House, having been the headquarters of the Nuffield Foundation, has also reverted to private ownership, as has the Holme. On Park Road, Abbey Lodge, another villa by Decimus Burton dating from the late 1820s, was demolished in 1928 and replaced by a block of flats, speeding the decline of Park Road from its earlier pretensions to gentility.

Regent's College, the successor to Bedford College on the site of the main farm in Marylebone Park and then of South Villa. Bedford College expanded rapidly from 1908. Various new buildings were added, designed by, among others, Basil Champneys and Maxwell Ayrton. The best of a mixed bag is the library by S.R.J. Smith (1912–13).

Near the top of Albany Street, once separated from each other by the Cumberland Market branch of the Regent's Canal, are two of Nash's most distinctive developments. The two Park Villages are reminiscent of the ten varied model cottages Nash had built at Blaise Castle near Bristol in 1811, considered by Pevsner 'the *ne plus ultra* of the Picturesque Movement'. On a semicircular road north of the barracks is Park Village West, begun by Nash and completed by James Pennethorne. A series of small villas,

each one distinctive in its own style but set close together, Park Village West was the prototype of countless other garden estates. Nash, who here was both architect and developer, lavished more care on the details of the houses than on some of the grander buildings in the park. Of a second set of villas, Park Village East, only part remains. The eastern range, including the whole of Serpentine Road, was demolished when the London to Birmingham railway widened its tracks between 1900 and 1906.

Park Village West (1823–34). Nash himself designed and developed two sets of villas, each of them individually detailed, making villages on either side of the Cumberland Market branch of the Regent's Canal. They were completed by his architectural heir, James Pennethorne. These Picturesque villas, set among trees, exerted a strong influence on the subsequent development of the middle-class suburb in England.

Tower House, Park Village West. The most distinctive of the houses in either of the two park villages, Tower House, in an Italianate style and with its porch heightened into an octagonal tower, was built for James Johnson, doctor both to Nash himself and to William IV. Subsequent inhabitants have included W.P. Frith, the painter of *Derby Day*, and the designer Norman Hartnell.

5

PARKLAND

The imposing presence of the terraces and villas of Regent's Park is achieved as much by their setting as by their architecture. They are part of a deliberate landscape set halfway between country and town. Here, however, instead of a park surrounding a house, the terraces surround and define the park. This in turn makes a setting for the villas and for the Inner Circle at its heart. The park has other features typical of country houses: entrance lodges with imposing gates, parkland, avenues of trees, lakes with ornamental waterfowl, formal gardens, fountains and sculpture. It has a central axis in the Broad Walk and other set paths, as well as a mixture of lawn, meadowland, wetland and woodland. At no point is it possible to see from one side of the park to the other.

The soil underlying Regent's Park is London clay, a layer of over 200 feet above chalk, with gravel only on its southern border. The park rises gently from south to north. It has a low plateau in the Inner Circle and a ridge along the line of the Broad Walk, forming a separate spine. With 410 acres of land, its highest point is at the Readymoney Fountain, at 138 feet, and its lowest area, at 82 feet, runs along the southern edge of the park. There are four and a half miles of road in the park, eighty-seven miles of walks, thirteen bridges and three tunnels – two in the Zoo and one under the Marylebone Road, connecting the gardens of Park Crescent and Park Square.

Virtually nothing remains of the original Marylebone Park, as the entire park was landscaped by Nash between 1811 and 1816. Although grazing continued after this date, with sheep keeping the grass short until the First World War, the work removed not only the buildings in the park but also the banks and hedges between the fields, and the tracks running across them. Such trees as existed were felled in preparation for replanting. In its early years, the park often resembled a building site more than a place of recreation.

Not only has Marylebone Park vanished, little of Nash's own parkland can now be seen, as nearly all of it has been

The Readymoney Fountain (1869) was the gift of a wealthy Parsee, Sir Cowasjee Jehangir, who, in gratitude to the British Raj for its protection of the Parsees, in 1865 sent £1200 from India to pay for a fountain 'in The Regent's Park or Kensington where a large number of nobility or gentry frequent'. Twenty-two feet high, and recently restored, it is made of Sicilian marble and Aberdeen granite. On its sides are reliefs of Victoria, Albert and Sir Cowasjee, as well as a lion and a Brahmin bull. 'Readymoney' refers to the donor's profession as a moneylender.

The park in autumn: looking past the children's boating pond towards the main lake.

Scenes on and around the lake. The lake has not always been benign. On 15 January 1867, the ice broke under the weight of the skaters on it, plunging 150 people into its waters. Forty of them died.

changed or renewed. Two principal features that remain are the lake and the canal. The lake had been dug by 1816, with the spoil spread over the surrounding parkland. With three branches and six small islands, it remains the park's main ornament. Its success as a Picturesque illusion was noted by a German traveller, Prince Hermann von Pückler-Muskau: 'You imagine you see a broad river flowing through luxuriant banks and going off in the distance in several arms; while in fact you are looking upon a small piece of standing, though clear, water created by art and labour'. The lake was situated in the existing valley of the Tyburn, from which its water originally came.

BELOW LEFT A grey squirrel. Other mammals in the park outside the Zoo include foxes, five species of bat and the hedgehog, otherwise a rarity in central London. Sadly, an attempt to reintroduce the red squirrel into the park in the late 1970s met with failure.

BELOW RIGHT Greylag geese, one of the eleven species of geese in Regent's Park's waterfowl collection.

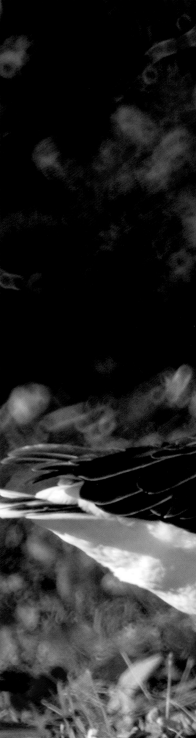

The towpath of the Regent's Canal provides an attractive walk as it passes through the park, running from St John's Wood, through the Zoo, to the basin at Water Meeting Bridge which was once the departure point of the 'Collateral Cut', the Cumberland Market branch of the canal.

Once deeper than it is today, up to 13 feet, the lake was made shallower following a serious skating accident in 1867, when forty people died. The grass used to run down to the lake, but heavy use has meant that the edge of the lake has now been hardened.

Nash was actively involved in the Regent's Canal, intended to join the terminus of the Grand Junction Canal at Paddington to the Thames at Limehouse. There had been a number of earlier projects for such a canal, including one, by Thomas Homer, running through the south of Marylebone Park. When Homer learnt that the Duke of Portland's leases on the park were about to fall in, he arranged a meeting with Nash and from that point the canal became a feature of the plans for the park. Originally, Nash thought of running the canal through the middle of the park and linking it to the lake. Problems with access through the neighbouring Portman Estate, and the commissioners' misgivings about allowing industrial barges near the villas, led Nash to reroute the canal through a wide cutting to the north of the park. This cutting was dug in 1812, by men under the contractors Hugh McIntosh and Samuel Jones, when its banks were planted with shrubs to consolidate them. The main bridge over the canal, named Macclesfield Bridge after the chairman of the canal company, the Earl of Macclesfield, was the scene of the most dramatic incident in the nineteenth-century history of the park. On 2 October 1874, the *Tilbury*, a barge carrying gunpowder, exploded early in the morning, killing the three members of her crew, badly damaging the bridge and frightening the animals in the Zoo. It also wrecked the Park Superintendent's house, which was rebuilt on the Inner Circle.

Much of what is in the modern-day park was not intended by Nash. He had no thought of creating large open spaces of grass, and certainly none of providing grounds for organized sport. He had no plans for formal gardens, as his vision was far closer in sympathy to the aristocratic parks of the eighteenth century than to the

RIGHT Looking across St Mark's Bridge towards the Broad Walk. The bridge replaces a suspension bridge constructed over the canal in 1843, after the opening of Primrose Hill to the public.

BELOW The decision to reroute the Regent's Canal through the north of Regent's Park was taken to keep the canal away from the villas. Now that the canal, no longer an industrial artery, has become an ornamental feature, it has been used to enhance the appeal of the modern Quinlan Terry villas built between 1988 and 2004 on its banks. Looking east towards the backs of Hanover Lodge and of Ionic, Veneto, Gothick and Corinthian Villas.

Three of the six Quinlan Terry villas above the Regent's Canal and reflected in its waters. From left to right: Regency Villa, Veneto Villa and Ionic Villa. The other new villas are Corinthian Villa, Gothick Villa and Tuscan Villa. The backs of these villas, with gardens running down to the canal, are more successful than their fronts, which are crowded together along the Outer Circle. The decision to build the villas on parkland was controversial, as the land, freed by the demolition of a block of student accommodation attached to Hanover Lodge, might otherwise have been given back to the park.

display gardens of the nineteenth. He was even opposed to the planting of shrubs, decreeing that these should only be allowed in the immediate proximity of the villas. The main planting of the park was to be of trees, which would control the views.

For the first twenty-four years of the existence of the park, popular access to it was restricted to its main roads, the Inner and Outer Circles, and to the roads between them. Entrance to the main body of the park was reserved to the owners of the terraces and villas, and 'to those of the Public to whom it should be thought proper to give keys'. Mirroring this, there were two societies in the park, the Zoological Society (from 1828) and the Royal Botanic Society (from 1838), whose grounds were open only to fellows and their guests, while from 1832 another area was reserved for the archery of members of the Royal Toxophilite Society. In addition, the villas were surrounded by substantial private grounds and many of the terraces also had private gardens.

The commissioners had decided to bring the building programme to an end in 1826. In 1832, however, they asked Nash to prepare a plan suggesting how the eastern side of the park could be made accessible to the public. Nash's response was his final plan of the park. On it the Prince Regent's guinguette has disappeared, there are no terraces except outside the Outer Circle, and the number of main villas has dropped to eight. Also, instead of the private drive leading to the guinguette, the southern part of the Broad Walk, the future spine of the park, is shown for the first time, planted as an avenue.

Three years after the Great Reform Act of 1832, and following the report of the Commission on Public Walks in the following year, eighty-eight acres on the eastern side of the park and along the canal were finally opened to the public. This was followed by in 1841 by ninety-two acres in the main northern area of the park. That year also saw the purchase of Primrose Hill, to protect the northern views from the park and to reduce the pressure for public access on the remaining closed areas of Regent's Park.

A set of eighteen watercolours by Charles Anderson, dating from around 1870, gives the best impression of life in the park in mid-Victorian times. Here Decimus Burton's Colosseum, with the tower of Sir John Soane's Holy Trinity to its right, is seen from near the Broad Walk across the English Garden. The railings on the sides of the paths indicate the restrictions imposed on visitors to the park at the time.

The opening of the rest of the park was a slow process and is still incomplete today. Even after 1841, 135 acres of parkland remained closed. This private area was reduced by the opening to the public in 1883 of what had been a subscription garden, serving the tenants of Cornwall, Clarence, Sussex and Hanover Terraces, which had blocked access to the south of the lake. Although hotly contested by the terrace leaseholders, the question drew the attention of the Liberal Prime Minister, William Gladstone. From this point it became official policy to return land to the park when the leases of the villas in the park came up for renewal, as they did between 1916 and 1932. Only Winfield House now keeps substantial private grounds.

During the later years of the nineteenth century, and the early years of the twentieth, the park took on many of its modern aspects. The Broad Walk was extended in 1863, when the Avenue Garden replaced its southern stretch, and between 1865 and 1867 the English Garden was added to its east. A major loss, however, was that of the Colosseum in 1875, demolished in the lifetime of its architect, Decimus

Burton, and replaced by Cambridge Gate. What the park was like in this period can best be seen in a fine series of contemporary paintings by the artist Charles Anderson.

The park also acquired many of its minor buildings during this period, to add to Nash's original lodges. The oldest one surviving is the refreshment lodge immediately to the north of Chester Road, originally one of a pair. A refreshment room opened half way up the Broad Walk in 1879. There were, however, no playgrounds in the park in the nineteenth century. The first concession to children was a sandpit on Marylebone Green in 1911. Subsequently, playgrounds were established here, at Gloucester and Hanover Gates, and on Primrose Hill. The popularity of the park was recognized by gifts to it of sculpture, including fountains, notably the Readymoney Fountain at the crest of the Broad Walk, near to the site of the first bandstand.

The park was used for allotments in the First World War, with a military camp and parade grounds. While it survived the war largely unscathed, little maintenance was done, leading to many flowerbeds being grassed over. The effects of the Second World War were far more severe.

The Broad Walk, the avenue forming the main axis of the park, was originally intended to lead to the Prince Regent's villa. It extended Nash's route from Westminster beyond Portland Place. The interruption to the route posed by the gardens of Park Crescent and Park Square is one of the obstacles facing Sir Terry Farrell's 2008 proposal for a 'Nash Ramblas' walk leading from Primrose Hill to Westminster.

To the east of the Broad Walk, looking towards Cumberland Green. The Broad Walk was extended northwards to the Outer Circle in 1863. Its southern end was replaced between 1863 and 1865 by the Avenue Garden.

Apart from renewed 'Dig for Victory' allotments, and the production of hay to feed the Zoo animals, much of the park was taken over by the military, with a large area of huts on Cumberland Green. The iron railings that had replaced the original oak palings around the park were removed and many trees felled. Anti-glider trenches were dug on the sports fields and air-raid shelters in the east side of the park, and there were a number of barrage balloon emplacements. The buildings in and around the park also suffered heavily from bomb damage. The resulting rubble was piled up in the park and subsequently spread to the depth of 10 feet across the northern sports pitches, adding to the difficulties of draining and maintaining them. This explains why in the modern park the northern playing fields are at a higher level than the Zoo. In the process, what was left of the valley of the Tyburn was obliterated.

There are also, of course, the business areas of the park. The main working area is the Storeyard, on the corner of the Inner Circle and Chester Road, which contains the offices of the Park Manager and other staff, including the Royal Parks Constabulary. The stabling, however, is no longer used and nothing is now grown from seed in the greenhouses, with flowers being imported from Hyde Park and held in Regent's Park until needed. Instead, the area is used by Capel College to teach horticulture and park management. Part of the land that once surrounded Holford House is now the Leafyard, and there is also a working area inside the Inner Circle facing the Storeyard.

Regent's Park is, however, nowadays the breeding centre for waterfowl in the Royal Parks. A Nature Study and Waterfowl Centre, with its own short stretch of lake, was built near Hanover Island in 1992. Here a great variety of waterfowl are hatched. Some are then sent to other royal parks or traded with outside customers. The islands in the lake are inaccessible to visitors to the park, while the fenced-off meadow to the east of the Long Bridge allows ducks, geese and swans to live undisturbed.

Reminiscent of a temple, the Hub is intended as a Picturesque addition to the park. Ninety per cent of its floor space is below ground, providing changing rooms for sporting activities. On its mound is a circular café with a 360° degree view over the surrounding parkland.

BELOW Organized games now dominate the open area of grass south of the Zoo, especially at weekends. Regent's Park has become the largest open-air venue for sport in central London.

BOTTOM Recent fencing around Park Square.

Although not one of its original purposes, sport now plays a major part in the park's activities. Cricket, football, rugby and hockey have all been played since the 1870s, particularly on Cumberland Green and the main open area to the south of the Zoo. A recent drainage campaign has made these areas far more usable for games. A purpose-built new pavilion on a new site, the Hub, has replaced the previous Bernhard Baron Pavilion.

The fencing around the park is not now the original oak paling, which helped give it a rustic feeling. The park is now surrounded by metal fencing and a thick hedge, mainly of privet. While a substantial boundary is nowadays necessary to keep out the noise and visual disturbance caused by traffic on the park roads, it has diminished the connection between the park and the terraces that surround it, an effect increased by the height of some of the trees near the boundary of the park and in front of the terraces.

Very little of Nash's own planting has survived, partly due to the problems caused by poorly drained soil. The effects of formal planting can, however, still be seen on the Broad Walk, between Chester Road and Readymoney Fountain, with its avenue of trees on the east and west. Nash's own preference was for native and standard exotic trees. The more unusual plantings were later, reflecting the Victorian interest in trees from around the Empire. As well as the drainage problem, the trees in the park have suffered from ravages during the two world wars, Dutch Elm Disease and the storm of 1987.

A surprisingly large number of species of birds, from the common to the highly unusual, visit the park, though both resident and migrant species have altered over the years, reflecting changes in the national bird population. The herons, nesting in their heronry on one of the islands on the boating lake, are in fact a relatively recent arrival. Rarities also sometimes put in an appearance, but none has provoked as much public interest as the escape of Goldie the golden eagle from the Zoo, and his evasion of capture for twelve days, in 1965.

Some of the many waterfowl in Regent's Park (clockwise from top left): a grey heron stands on a vent of the Bakerloo Line, which runs under the lake, with a coot's nest below; a coot and its chick; a mute swan; a black swan; Canada geese; red-crested pochards; and a shelduck, a bar-headed goose and a red-crested pochard. In all there are sixty species of waterfowl in the park, including three species of swans and eleven of geese. To limit the depredations of foxes, which have been active in the park since the late 1970s, many of their eggs are now incubated and hatched at the Waterfowl Centre.

6

GARDENS

John Nash, in contrast to his one-time partner Humphry Repton, who often included garden schemes in his landscaping plans, made no provision for gardens in Regent's Park. In it he was far more concerned with trees than flowers, deprecating the introduction of shrubs and opposing the establishment of private gardens for the terraces. Gardens, however, soon started to appear in the park, both around the villas and in front of the terraces.

In 1824, after plans for a grand circus – or a villa for the Duke of Wellington – in the centre of the park had been abandoned, the eighteen acres of land inside the Inner Circle were leased to Messrs Jenkins and Gwither of Lisson Grove, who had supplied most of the trees for the park. Nothing of the market garden Jenkins established there survives, with the possible exception of a few plane trees. Then in 1838 the land was leased to the recently founded Botanic Society of London – from 1839 the Royal Botanic Society. The society announced a competition for the design of its new gardens. This was won by Robert Marnock and Decimus Burton, whose design was arranged round a new central avenue, running from south to north. They created the lake, using the spoil to make the mounds in the centre of the gardens, and laid out a variety of winding paths between specialized gardens. In 1845, the society also commissioned Decimus Burton to design a large conservatory at the end of its central axis. Built by Turner of Dublin, also responsible for the Palm House at Kew, the conservatory held a range of tropical flowers, including the Victoria Regis lily, on which the Secretary could sit in a chair. The society held annual flower shows in giant marquees. Queen Victoria was a regular attender, bringing the royal children. Another visitor was Elizabeth Barrett, from nearby Wimpole Street, who picked flowers in the garden to give to Robert Browning.

The layout of the society's gardens was not static. There were changes and additions over the next ninety years. Dependent, however, on its private members for income, and excluding the general public, the society never solved

The oriental poppy, *Papaver orientale*, not to be confused with the opium poppy, *Papaver somniferum*. In nature the oriental poppy is a brilliant scarlet, tinged with orange, but selective breeding has led to the development of a wide range of colours.

The suitably hidden entrance to St John's Lodge Garden, 'a garden fit for meditation', looking out towards the Inner Circle.

BELOW Looking down the central axis of Queen Mary's Gardens towards the Triton Fountain, through the wrought-iron gates given by Sigismund Goetze to celebrate the Silver Jubilee of George V and Queen Mary in 1935.

OPPOSITE AND ON PAGES 72–73 Some of the thirty thousand roses of four hundred varieties on show in Queen Mary's Gardens. Although this series of gardens contains many other plants, including the national collection of delphiniums and nine thousand begonias, the roses are always the main attraction.

a number of problems. Run by a coterie, with the original secretary, James Sowerby, being succeeded by his son and then grandson, it was better at putting on social events than at innovative horticulture. It was not a scientific body, was poorly managed and was always short of funds. This led to tired-looking floral displays, not helped by the heavy clay soil of the park and the sulphur from the many coal fires of Victorian London. When the society surrendered its lease in 1930, the land reverted to the crown.

Although a number of other uses were suggested for it, including a folk museum, the Inner Circle was taken over by the Department of Works and laid out by the Park Superintendent, Duncan Campbell, with much

encouragement and advice from the artist Sigismund Goetze, who lived at Grove House. It opened as a public garden in April 1932. Burton's conservatory, found to be past repair, was pulled down. Two magnificent wrought iron gates, both gifts from Goetze, were placed at its entrances: the one facing Chester Road in 1933; the other, at the head of the central avenue, in 1935, the year of George V's silver jubilee, when the reconfigured garden was formally named Queen Mary's Gardens.

Goetze was profuse in gifts of his own work, and that of others, at times to the point of embarrassment. He painted the Locarno Rooms in the Foreign Office with scenes of the British Empire, for which he did not charge.

His offer to paint the ceiling of the Reading Room of the British Museum was, however, refused. Besides the gates, he gave many of the sculptures inside the gardens, as well as the original cherry trees on Chester Road. He also gave the pool at the top of the avenue in Queen Mary's Gardens in 1939, just before his death. After the war, in 1950, his widow, Constance, donated the Triton group in the fountain, by William McMillan, in his memory.

Not all of the Royal Botanic Society's layout disappeared in the reconfiguration, as the central axis, the lake and the mounds remain, as well as Nursery Lodge on the Inner Circle. There are also remnants of its displays, notably the fossilized tree stumps to the north of the lake. The principal innovation in the new garden, giving it its alternative name of the Rose Garden, was a concentration on roses, with the trellises for the rosary being given, inevitably, by Goetze.

In 1932 Sydney Carroll put on *Twelfth Night* in the gardens. The success of this led to the establishment of the Open Air Theatre, officially the New Shakespeare Company. Since 1933, when an enclosed performance area with permanent staging was first used, the company has presented a season of Shakespeare plays, interspersed with other plays and musicals, every year. During the 1944 season, it was a matter of honour for actors on stage to ignore V1s flying overhead. Undoubtedly the play most frequently performed has been *A Midsummer Night's Dream*, but many other plays have been successfully produced. On a balmy evening, with the light fading and darkness lending magic to a good production, there are few experiences more enjoyable.

Very different from the informal paths and variety of Queen Mary's Garden, the Avenue Garden was created by William Andrews Nesfield between 1863 and 1865. Nesfield was the leading British garden designer of his day, often working with the architect Anthony Salvin. Much admired by Prince Albert, Nesfield had been responsible for the garden layout outside Decimus Burton's Palm House

The Triton Fountain, given by
Constance Goetze in memory of her
husband, Sigismund. The sculpture is
by William McMillan RA, who won the
Gold Medal of the Royal Society of
Arts for it in 1950. The central figure,
half human and half fish, is Triton, the
son of Poseidon, the god of the sea.
Flanked by two fish-tailed nereids,
he blows the principal jet of water
upwards from a conch shell. Other jets
issue from the mouths of fishes.

LEFT A fountain in the Avenue Garden in snow.

BELOW Crocuses to the east of the Avenue Garden.

at Kew. In all, he was responsible for work on the gardens of over 250 estates, including those of Alton Towers and Castle Howard. He specialized in grand gardens, reviving the formal box and gravel parterres of the seventeenth and early eighteenth centuries.

The Avenue Garden, also known as the Italian Garden, replaced Nash's original avenue of trees between Park Square and Chester Road, which by the 1860s was in poor condition. Nesfield kept two of the four lines of trees, with elms outside horse chestnuts. Inside these, he set a series of highly ornate display beds, punctuated by tazzas and urns, to both sides of a plain central avenue.

Although the garden was much applauded and visited on its completion, Nesfield's work as a whole went out of fashion before his death in 1881, when a taste for the more natural gardens associated with William Robinson, and subsequently Gertrude Jekyll, came into vogue. Although well maintained until the First World War, the garden was then allowed to decline until a major restoration was carried out, with the help of a Lottery grant, between 1993 and 1996. Only a few of the Victorian tazzas and urns survived to be incorporated into the new garden. These had, however, come when new from the Marylebone firm of Austin and Seeley. Replacements, copied from the firm's catalogue, were made out of the same artificial limestone used in the nineteenth century. Eight fountains, from the catalogue, were added, even though the original gardens had had no fountains. The elms and horse chestnuts flanking the garden were replaced by limes.

Parallel to the Avenue Garden, and often unnoticed by visitors to the park, is the English Garden. Created by Nesfield's son, Markham Nesfield, between 1865 and 1867 as a contrast to the Avenue Garden, it incorporates meandering paths and an artificial mound, with shrubs and informal planting. It was also restored in the 1990s, although the trees that make part of it are more prominent than Markham Nesfield – who was killed in a riding accident in Regent's Park in 1874 – intended. This area of the park, which for a time had its own small lake and now also contains a Bog Garden, was once dominated by Decimus Burton's Colosseum, which had its own gardens on the Outer Circle.

The least expected of all the public gardens in the park is St John's Lodge Garden. The garden was once larger than it is now and bordered meadowland running down to the lake. The third Marquess of Bute, who wanted 'a garden fit for meditation', commissioned it from the Scottish architect Robert Weir Schultz in 1891. A sunken garden was reached from the entrance front of the villa with steps then leading up to a pool, once with a statue of St John but now with one of Hylas and the Nymph. From here a stone loggia, now a pergola, led to an oval lawn, used for tennis and surrounded by pleached limes, and finally to a nymphaeum – now a covered seat. In 1928 the garden, then entered via the lodge of St John's Villa, was opened to the public. It was restored in 1994, but reduced in size, when a new entrance was made directly from the Inner Circle.

These main public gardens are by no means all of those in the park, even if the 'Zoological Gardens', as the Zoo was known for 150 years, are excluded. At the north-east there is a Winter Garden, on either side of the paths leading from the Charlbert Street entrance.

CLOCKWISE FROM RIGHT The pergola, framing the pool and the view towards St John's Lodge; *Hylas and the Nymph*, statue by H.A. Pegram RA (1933): Hylas, beloved by Hercules, was dragged down beneath the water by an enamoured nymph; the entrance lawn near the pool and stable block.

The lake in Queen Mary's Gardens dates back to the days of its predecessor, the Royal Botanic Society, which laid out the gardens on a scheme by Robert Marnock and Decimus Burton in the early 1840s. The spoil from the lake then excavated was used to create the mounds in the garden. Here the stream runs down via a cascade towards the lake.

At the western end of the lake in Queen Mary's Gardens is Alpine Island, reached by a hump-backed wooden bridge. The island, formed by large boulders with pockets of scree, dates from the days of the Royal Botanic Society, though at one time there was a second bridge connecting the island to the northern shore of the lake. The rock garden on the island combines typical alpine plants with Japanese plants and trees.

TOP LEFT Looking across to Alpine Island past a silver birch, *Betula pendula*.

TOP RIGHT *Cornus controversa* 'Variegata' is the most striking tree on Alpine Island. This Japanese dogwood is commonly known as the wedding cake tree, because of its tiered branches.

BELOW To the left of the wedding cake tree is a stone lantern, a gift from Sigismund Goetze, who bought it at the Chelsea Flower Show in 1936.

LEFT, ABOVE Looking east from York Bridge over the least visited part of the lake. The area around this arm of the lake is deliberately left uncultivated.

LEFT, BELOW Between the lake and the York Bridge tennis courts lies the Wildlife Garden, aimed at educating children about the creation and preservation of different habitats, including grasses. Over recent years areas of meadowland have been left uncut in the park and ten thousand wild flowers have been planted.

In the south of the park there is a Community Wildlife Garden, bordering the lake near York Bridge. More like those of a London square than parts of a park, the gardens of Park Square and Park Crescent are joined underneath the Euston Road by the Nannies' Tunnel, where nursemaids were rumoured to have kept unobserved assignations with soldiers from the Albany Street barracks. There are private gardens, outside the Outer Circle, in front of Chester, Cumberland and Gloucester Terraces, and a substantial lawn in front of Sussex Place. Grove House, the Holme and St John's Lodge also have their own gardens, as do the new Quinlan Terry villas on the canal bank and Regent's College. The most unusual garden is that belonging to the Royal College of Physicians in front of the terrace of houses in St Andrews Place. All the plants here were listed in the *Pharmacopoeia Londiniensis* of 1618 as being of medicinal value. The finest private garden in the park, however, is undoubtedly that of Winfield House, the home of the American Ambassador. At over twelve acres, it is the second largest garden in central London after that of Buckingham Palace, providing the house with its own parkland. The house itself is set at the centre of a series of gardens designed to give pleasure throughout the year.

BELOW The medicinal garden of the Royal College of Physicians, in St Andrews Place, reflects the use of plants in the treatment of disease since classical times. With almost a thousand different species on display during the year, the garden includes plants which have provided the basis for modern drugs – such as *Digitalis lanata*, the woolly foxglove, used in the treatment of heart disease – as well as those that would now simply be seen as poisonous.

BOTTOM Two hellebores: *Helleborus* x *nigercors* (left) and *Helleborus* x *hybridus* (right). In the past, hellebore was used as a purgative to treat melancholy, epilepsy, leprosy and internal worms – a dangerous course, as all hellebores are poisonous.

7

THE ZOO

The Zoo dates from early in the history of Regent's Park, although it formed no part of Nash's original plans. It looks out on the rest of the park and can be seen from it, whether from the Outer Circle as it passes through the Zoo, the Broad Walk, the main playing area or the top of Primrose Hill. The Regent's Canal, no longer used for commercial traffic and open to the public, divides the Zoo, allowing walkers and those on boats a fine view of the animals in the canalside enclosures as well as the birds in the Snowdon Aviary.

The initiative to start a society dedicated to the study of wild animals came from Sir Thomas Stamford Raffles, a distinguished servant of the East India Company and the founder of Singapore, who spent his adult life in the Far East. A dedicated collector of wild life, he drew up plans to 'establish a Society bearing the same relation to Zoology and the animal kingdom that the Horticultural Society bears to Botany and the vegetable kingdom' on his return to England in 1824. Initially attracting 151 subscribers, each paying £3 to join, the new society was established in 1826 with Raffles as its first president. With its gardens first opened in 1828, it received a royal charter in 1829 but remains a private society.

Originally the society hoped to lease the land inside the Inner Circle. Instead, it was granted the lease, at eighteen

LEFT Sumatran tiger (*Panthera tigris sumatrae*), the smallest and darkest member of the tiger family, and one of the most endangered. An inhabitant of the rain forest, its habitat has shrunk drastically as a consequence of felling for land cultivation. The conditions in which tigers live in the Zoo are a great improvement on the bare cages of Victorian times, but there are current plans to improve them further.

RIGHT Superb starling (*Spreo superbus*), a native of East Africa. Its numbers have declined because of loss of habitat and the use of chemical pest control.

guineas for the first three years, of five acres in the north of the park. This soon increased to twenty acres on both sides of the Outer Circle. The area acquired, originally intended for barracks, had become available when the site of the barracks was moved to Albany Street.

Nowadays, when zoos are common across the world, it is hard to realize the originality of the new society. It was the first society in the world dedicated to the collection and scientific study of animals. Indeed its title, the Zoological Society of London, shortened to Zoo, gave this word to the English and then to all other languages. It later had the first reptile house in the world (1849), the first aquarium (1853) and the first insect house (1881), as well as establishing the world's first 'park zoo' at its second site at Whipsnade in Bedfordshire (1931). London Zoo soon became the largest collection of wild animals in the world, as well as being the most important centre of knowledge of them and having the finest specialist zoological library.

In keeping with its status as part of Regent's Park, many of the early buildings, some echoing the Nash terraces, were designed by Decimus Burton, who also planned the Zoo's initial layout. Few of these buildings have survived, being replaced by houses better suited to animals. A misguided conception that tropical animals would be unable to withstand the English winter led to the early tropical houses having no external runs. Burton's Giraffe House, built in 1837, in an adapted form still serves its original purpose.

For the first eighteen years after the Zoo opened in 1828 entrance was only available to fellows of the society and their guests. In this restriction of entry it echoed other areas of Regent's Park, not only the Royal Botanic Society in the Inner Circle but also the private grounds and gardens attached to the villas and terraces. The income from the fellowship was, however, insufficient to fund the many calls on the Zoo's income. This led to the general opening of the Zoo to all paying customers in 1846, with fellows retaining only the privilege of Sunday entrance.

The first animals in the Zoo came from the royal menageries at the Tower and at Windsor, from Raffles's own collection and from private donations. Soon, animals were arriving from all over the world but principally the British Empire. The collection was by no means restricted to mammals, with birds, fish, reptiles and insects forming parts of the display. Nor were all the early exhibits alive. There was a large collection of stuffed animals, finally transferred to form the nucleus of the Natural History Museum.

From the beginning the Zoo thrived on star attractions, including the first four giraffes, Selim, Mabrouk, Zaida and Guib-allah, Tony the chimpanzee and Obaysch, the first hippo seen in Europe since the fall of the Roman Empire. The Zoo also contained animals which subsequently became extinct, including the thylacine, the Tasmanian marsupial wolf. Another was the quagga, a relative of the zebra, the only existing photograph of which was taken in the Zoo.

There can be no doubt that, in all senses, the biggest star of the Victorian Zoo was Jumbo the African elephant. Born in the Sudan, Jumbo arrived in the Zoo in 1865. Eventually standing 11 feet high, for many years he gave rides to children. African elephants are, however, harder to train than their Indian cousins and mature male elephants are extremely dangerous during their periods of *musht*. Alarmed by the threat Jumbo represented, the Superintendent of the Zoo, Abraham Bartlett, was relieved to accept an offer of £2000 for Jumbo from the American showman Phineas T. Barnum in 1882.

The news of Jumbo's impending departure caused a national uproar, with thousands of children writing to Queen Victoria begging her to stop the sale. Much was made of Jumbo's coming separation from the Zoo's female elephant, Alice, represented as his wife even though the two had never mated. Jumbo reinforced the protests by refusing to enter the crate in which he was to be transported. Eventually he left for a hugely successful new career in

Jumbo with his keeper, Matthew Scott, who accompanied him to America. Jumbo's meteoric career was finally brought to an end when he was hit by an unscheduled freight train at St Thomas in Canada in 1885. His skeleton is preserved in the American Museum of Natural History in New York.

Penguin Pool, by Berthold Lubetkin of Tecton (1934), the best known of the Zoo's enclosures. While non-naturalistic, the pool avoids the appearance of caging. It no longer houses penguins.

America, giving his name to anything oversized – from crosswords and jets to hamburgers and headaches.

The popular interest in Jumbo mirrored the familiarity of Londoners with the Zoo and their affection for it. With large numbers of visitors, the area leased in Regent's Park eventually increased to thirty-six acres on both sides of the canal. New buildings, including the famous Lion House (1877), were added or slowly replaced the original buildings. The first half of the twentieth century saw the addition of the Mappin Terraces (1914), and of Berthold Lubetkin's Gorilla House (1932) and Penguin Pool (1934). While many of these enclosures and cages were too small to allow their inmates to behave in a natural way, the breeding record of the Zoo was impressive from its earliest days.

Nothing attracted more visitors than baby animals. Perhaps the most famous of these was Brumas, the first polar bear cub to be born in the Zoo, in 1950. Undoubtedly the greatest celebrities amongst the adult animals were the giant pandas, from Ming to Chi-Chi (visited by 25,000,000 people over fourteen years), Chia-Chia and Ching-Ching. Despite enormous efforts, including international courtship flights, the Zoo has yet to produce a giant panda baby.

One famous Zoo star left a lasting mark on children's literature. Winnie, a brown bear, was the regimental mascot of a Canadian regiment raised in Winnipeg during the First World War. Given to the Zoo after the war, Winnie was exceptionally tame, taking tins of her favourite mixture of golden syrup and condensed milk directly from children. One such enthralled visitor, brought by his father, was Christopher Robin Milne. After their visit, his father changed the name of the bear he was then writing about from Pooh to Winnie the Pooh.

The celebrity of the animals was greatly enhanced by programmes broadcast from the Zoo aimed at educating listeners and viewers, as well as entertaining them. Following pioneering radio broadcasts by L.G. Mainland between the wars, two of the best-known early television

BELOW LEFT Bactrian camels (*Camelus bactrianus*), native to the Gobi Desert, in front of what was built as the Elephant and Rhinoceros Pavilion, designed by Sir Hugh Casson (1965).

BELOW RIGHT Emus (*Dromaius novaehollandiae*), which cannot fly but which can run at over twenty-five miles an hour, in an arid enclosure simulating their native Australia. Behind them is one of the distinctive Mappin Terraces (1914), called after their donor, John Newton Mappin. The terraces used to house goats on the top levels and bears on the lower.

programmes, *Zoo Time*, presented by Desmond Morris, and *Zoo Quest*, David Attenborough's first television series, focused on individual animals in the Zoo.

A less reputable display was the Chimpanzees' Tea Party, hugely popular with the public but seen increasingly as a caricature of animal behaviour. In the 1960s the reputation of zoos, including London Zoo, also began to suffer from a perception that they imprisoned animals, and that those who went to see them were complicit in cruelty. Guy the gorilla, who died during a dental operation necessitated by years of being fed sweets by children, was perceived as a principal victim. The way forward was seen to be outside London in safari parks, such as the Zoological Society's own park at Whipsnade, or indeed on real safaris to Africa.

The Zoo stayed open during both world wars, although some animals were evacuated or put down, but structural damage from bomb damage during the Second World War put a severe burden on the Zoo's finances, a strain increased by the pressing need to bring the Zoo's ageing buildings and enclosures up to date. Despite a record attendance of over three million in 1950, numbers had dropped to little more than 1,250,000 by 1983. The Zoo's financial problems were masked for a time by new buildings made possible

BELOW LEFT Raven's cage, designed by Decimus Burton, 1829. Little or none of its original fabric remains, following war damage and reconstruction, though the design remains close to Burton's own. It is no longer used to house birds.

BELOW RIGHT The Snowdon Aviary (1962–64), made of aluminium and including two waterfalls, allows visitors to walk through rather than in front of a cage, while placing birds in a relatively naturalistic environment. Set on the north bank of the Regent's Canal, the aviary adds to the enjoyment of passing through the Zoo via the canal.

by government grants and by the generosity of individual donors, notably that of the developers Jack Cotton and Charles Clore. The new buildings included the Snowdon Aviary (1962–64), the Elephant and Rhino Pavilion (1965), designed by Sir Hugh Casson, and the Charles Clore Pavilion for Mammals (1967). By the early 1990s, however, the underlying financial position had become untenable. A plan to take in ten extra acres of parkland, although endorsed by Act of Parliament, was defeated by local opposition, a reflection of the Zoo's unpopularity at the time and a justifiable reaction to the loss of parkland. In addition, a proposal for nightly illuminations of model animals on the canal was widely seen as 'Disneyfication'. After the government rejected an application for long-term funding, the closure of the Zoo was announced for September 1992.

It was from this low point that the fortunes of the Zoo began to revive. A gift from the Emir of Kuwait of £1,000,000 staved off closure in the short term. Other gifts followed, notably £1,000,000 for the Children's Zoo from Lord Paul in memory of his daughter, Ambika. This reprieve allowed the Zoo to plan for its future, even though this initially involved staff cuts and a reduction in the number of animals on display. In the years that followed

Alpacas (*Vicugna pacos*) and their taller cousins, llamas (*Lama glama*), members of the camelid family from South America, sometimes spit but are otherwise popular inhabitants of the Children's Zoo.

the Zoo pioneered new ways of displaying animals that allowed them to be shown in landscaped settings and to behave more naturally. If fewer animals were exhibited, their conditions were better. At the same time, some of the larger animals, including elephants and bears, were moved to Whipsnade.

The Zoo also profited from a growing recognition of the role of zoos in preserving endangered species. In a world where their habitats, from the poles to the tropics, are being threatened or destroyed, the alternative for many animals to life in a zoo is not freedom but extinction. Conservation has now become the central purpose of the Zoo, working with others around the world at breeding endangered species. This new mission is linked, together with the Zoo's continued scientific work, with a growing emphasis on education and interaction with the animals, particularly aimed at children. The twin aims of conservation and education have informed new buildings in the Zoo. The Web of Life, built for the Millennium, demonstrates the intricate workings of biodiversity. Gorilla Kingdom allows visitors an intimate view of a family of these great apes interacting with each another.

Not all the Zoo's problems have been solved. It is still a considerable distance from the Underground, presenting families assuming that Regent's Park is the nearest station with a mile's walk before reaching the Zoo. The Slips car park, although essential in providing parking for visitors, constitutes an ugly blot on the north-east of the park. Nevertheless, the Zoo has successfully adapted to the twenty-first century. The oldest and historically most important zoo in the world, with ten buildings listed Grade I or Grade II, it contains a wide range of animal life presented humanely and intelligently.

Most Londoners, and millions more from the rest of Britain and the world, have visited this unique institution as children or as adults. Even today, in an age of superb filmed natural history documentaries, there is still no substitute for seeing live wild animals at close quarters. Simultaneously a leading scientific organisation, dedicated to the study and conservation of animal life, an educational establishment teaching children about animals, and a place of entertainment competing with London's many other attractions, the Zoo remains a remarkable part of the history and identity of Regent's Park.

Two female gorillas (*Gorilla gorilla gorilla*), Effie (top) and Mjukuu (below), in the Zoo's central exhibit, Gorilla Kingdom, a substantial indoor and outdoor enclosure for a family group of this endangered species. At close quarters these great apes exude an aura of serenity.

8

PRIMROSE HILL

North of Regent's Park, before the land begins its main ascent to Hampstead and Highgate, stands the nearest hill to the centre of London. Reaching only 206 feet high at its summit, elsewhere Primrose Hill would be unremarkable. It is its commanding position, overlooking the Zoo, Regent's Park and then the whole sweep of London, that makes it memorable.

The dramatic presence of Primrose Hill has led many people to wonder whether it is man-made, perhaps the site of an ancient burial. Whatever lies beneath its surface, Primrose Hill has long attracted visionaries. William Blake saw the Spiritual Sun on it. This was 'not like a golden disc the size of a guinea but like the innumerable company of the heavenly host crying "Holy, Holy, Holy"'. It was also the site of a key moment in the foundation of modern paganism, and an early step towards a revived Welsh

national identity. Edward Williams was a stonemason from Glamorgan. Under his bardic name, Iolo Morganwg, he was also a prolific editor and forger of Welsh literature. In September 1792 he proclaimed 'The *Gorsedd* of the Bards of Britain' on Primrose Hill. *Gorsedd*, meaning a high seat or mountain top in Welsh, was translated by Morganwg as 'sublime moot'. Those present recited bardic poems inside a circle of small stones set around a larger one. Primrose Hill is also, inevitably, on a number of significant ley lines.

In 1898 the world was saved, unexpectedly, on Primrose Hill. That year H.G. Wells, who had earlier lived in nearby Fitzroy Road, published *The War of the Worlds*, in which Martians land at seven sites around London, including Primrose Hill. They make short work of the late-Victorian army and soon have London in their power. Their war machines are invincible and they choke the waterways,

LEFT Primrose Hill. A separate park since 1842, when it was officially opened to the public, Primrose Hill is very different in character from its much larger neighbour. Unlike Regent's Park, it was neither planned nor landscaped. It has almost no buildings and is seldom used for events. It nevertheless has a strong identity of its own.

RIGHT Primrose Hill is separated from Regent's Park by Prince Albert Road, the Regent's Canal and the Outer Circle, as well as by the Zoo, marked here by the Snowdon Aviary, which borders the hill's southern boundary. In the hill's south-west corner there is a gymnasium, first opened in 1848.

including the Thames and the Regent's Canal, with a red weed. Primrose Hill is 'their main redoubt', where they ingest human victims, making queer hooting noises before feeding. There they are building a giant flying machine as their next step towards the conquest of the world. The world has no defence but is saved by a small but fatal Martian weakness: the invaders have no immunity to terrestrial bacteria and are all found dead.

In reality, Primrose Hill is formed of London clay. It is not the burial site of a king, nor of a giant, and remarkably few archaeological finds have been found near it, as the area was little inhabited before the nineteenth century (though the village of Rugmore, recorded in Domesday, may well have been nearby; perhaps on the site of the Zoo). The hill is also not pierced by tunnels, except to its north by the London to Birmingham railway, the first trunk line to enter London and a remarkable early feat of engineering dating from 1834. Originally Primrose Hill had a neighbour to its west, Barrow Hill, but this was flattened when the West Middlesex Reservoir was built on it in 1825.

Once part of the Middlesex Forest, Primrose Hill had lost nearly all its trees to felling by 1300, after which it was used for grazing, being divided by hedges into four fields, called Blue House, Primrose Hill, Rugmoor and Sheppard's Hill, by 1800. Although not part of Marylebone Park, Primrose Hill was at the end of a track leading through the park and, in the eighteenth century, was a popular place of excursion for Londoners. Refreshments were sold at the Chalk Farm Tavern, which acquired a reputation for rowdiness and was notorious as a meeting place of duellists. There was, however, no chalk there, the name Chalk Farm being derived from Chalcot, a 'cold settlement', with barns belonging to Lower Chalcot Farm being the only other buildings near by.

It was also the scene of a notorious murder in 1678. The discovery in 'a ditch on the south side of Primrose Hill' of the body of a Protestant magistrate, Sir Edmund Berry Godfrey, was the trigger for the national paranoia of the Popish Plot, with public hysteria directed against Catholics.

Although Godfrey's body was transfixed by his own sword, he had in fact been strangled elsewhere. Three men were wrongly convicted and hanged for his murder, and many Catholics were also executed for imaginary treason, but the true facts of the case remain hidden.

One hundred and fifty years later Primrose Hill was threatened with the danger of becoming London's largest cemetery. The pioneer cemetery campaigner George Carden made it his first choice as the site for a London version of Père Lachaise in Paris. One of the plans submitted to Carden's cemetery company was even more spectacular. Thomas Willson's plan, exhibited in 1824, was for a necropolis: a brick pyramid, taller than St Paul's Cathedral, holding 5,167,104 bodies and covering eighteen acres. Although the cost was estimated at the then astronomical sum of £2,583,552, Willson nevertheless projected a profit of £10,764,800 made from selling the vaults at between £500 and £100 each.

Eton College, the owner of nearly all the hill and of a substantial estate to its north, had no wish for a cemetery on its land. It, nevertheless, at one point drew up a plan dividing the hill, and the rest of its estate, into building plots. The college did not find it easy, however, to attract builders. Primrose Hill was protected by its slopes, which would have made building more expensive than on the flat, and by its soil, a 'bed of very rank clay ... unfavourable for habitations'. It was also thought to be 'not at all desirable from the howling of the Beasts in the Zoological Gardens and the constant hissing and noise from the Railway'. The college could also see that leaving part of its estate open, with access across open fields to Regent's Park, would enhance the value of the rest of its land.

In the 1830s there was public pressure on the government to open more of Regent's Park to the public. To satisfy this demand, without encroaching on the land around the park villas, and to keep the northern view from the park open, the Treasury decided to buy Primrose Hill in 1837. The decision was given urgency by a renewed threat,

Trees on Primrose Hill. The trees in the hedges that made up the boundaries between the fields were cut down soon after the acquisition of Primrose Hill. Many of the trees planted in the 1880s were, in turn, cut down just before or during the Second World War. The poet Louis Macneice, who lived nearby, wrote during the Munich crisis of 1938, 'I found the Territorials hastily, inefficiently, cutting down the grove on the top of Primrose Hill.' Coming back to London soon afterwards, Macneice found 'Primrose Hill was embarrassingly naked, as if one's grandfather had shaved his beard off.'

posed by the North Metropolitan Cemetery Company, to turn the hill into a cemetery. The company's plan aroused widespread opposition both outside and inside Parliament. A strip of land at the eastern foot of the hill was bought by the crown from its owner, Lord Southampton, when he auctioned his sizeable nearby holdings in August 1840. After lengthy negotiations, in 1841 Eton then exchanged Primrose Hill for crown land in Eton itself not previously owned by the college. In 1842, following an Act of Parliament, Primrose Hill became a public park.

The acquisition of the land from Lord Southampton meant that the roads bordering the east of the new park, Regent's Park Road and Albert Terrace, had housing only on one side, leaving the view of the hill open. To the south, where two roads, the canal and the Zoo prevented an easy or natural link between the two parks, the view was also not blocked by housing. When later, in the 1870s, Primrose Hill Road was built over the eastern side of the hill, the road ran along the outside of the park. Only to the north, where until the 1890s Elsworthy Road ended in a cricket ground, and to the west, where the gardens of the houses of the Eyre Estate backed on to the park, were there no views of the hill.

In the early years after it became a park, when it was still situated on the edge of London, Primrose Hill remained rough open land, still used for grazing. It had no added amenities, other than boundary fencing and a new network of paths running between the gates, though a gymnasium was opened in 1848 and a refreshment lodge in 1862. The only house on Primrose Hill is the lodge at its south-western corner, dating from about 1860. Before the 1880s the hill had few trees, following the removal of boundary hedges between its original fields, although an oak was planted ceremoniously in 1864 to mark the tercentenary of Shakespeare's birth. Then in 1883, following an extensive drainage campaign, around five hundred trees were planted, including black poplar, hawthorn and ash, particularly on the north side of the hill.

Unlike Regent's Park, Primrose Hill has no gardens, and the only shrubs are in the border up its western side. While primroses were common on the hill into the nineteenth century, a succession of attempts to reintroduce them have largely failed, partly due to the removal of the hedges and banks on the south of the hill where they once flourished. Drainage has made games possible on its north-western side but the clay soil still encourages pools to form at the foot of the hill in wet weather.

Although used for allotments between 1914 and 1918, the park survived the First World War largely intact. Much more damage was done in the Second World War, when again there were allotments. Many of its trees were felled to make room for four anti-aircraft guns, near the top of the hill, with the area around them fenced off. A large part of the north-western area was made into a radar net. A barrage balloon was tethered near the playground and an air-raid shelter built at the hill's south-east corner. Primrose Hill was also hit by the only V2 to fall on either park. This landed near the reservoir in March 1945 and destroyed the refreshment lodge.

LEFT Primrose Hill at night. Unlike Regent's Park, Primrose Hill remains open at all times of day and night. The lamps, first erected in the 1850s, originally used gaslight and were lit individually each evening.

ABOVE RIGHT The keeper's lodge in the south-western corner of the hill has high chimneys, painted stone dressings and mullioned windows.

Primrose Hill panorama. Set amidst the multiple skyscrapers of modern London, older landmarks can still be seen, including the local St Mark's Church, St Pancras Station, St Paul's, Big Ben and the Victoria Tower. The obtrusive tower block in the centre is the thirty-six-storey Euston Tower (1963–70), near Warren Street, with Centre Point (1962–65) and the Telecom Tower (1961–65) to its right. Heavy use of the unofficial path directly up the front of the hill has led to scarring.

Since the war, Primrose Hill has resumed its function as a park, much favoured by dogs, picknickers and those wanting to enjoy the view over London. It is less used than Regent's Park for events, though made famous by David Bailey's photography and frequently used for filming. Unlike Regent's Park, it is open at all times, attempts to close it at night being successfully resisted by local inhabitants in 1975. The site of mass political meetings in the nineteenth century, and of a firework display to celebrate the end of the Crimean War, the hill drew huge crowds for spectacular 5 November firework displays for a number of years around the Millennium, until their popularity threatened public safety.

Above all, with a slope dropping sharply to its south, the top of the hill makes a superb viewing platform. Beyond the green spaces below, punctuated by the Snowdon Aviary and leading on to the main body of Regent's Park, can be seen a panorama of modern London: from Canary Wharf in the east to Westminster in the west and as far as Crystal Palace. In a view once dominated by the dome of St Paul's, this and other church towers are now overshadowed by modern skyscrapers, with the London Eye drawing attention to itself by its unusual shape. Although the Strategic Views Policy, otherwise known as the St Paul's Heights Code, has safeguarded this and other sightlines since the 1930s, the accretion of undistinguished and randomly sited tall buildings has sadly eaten into the clarity and appeal of the view. At least Primrose Hill remains a green space and its link with Regent's Park gives hope against the words of the prophetess Mother Shipton, 'When London surrounds Primrose Hill the streets of the Metropolis will run with blood.'

9

PLEASURES

Regent's Park is many things to many people. For a few it is their home, or their place of work or study. Others are regular or occasional visitors. People walk through it, from different points of entry and at different times of day, throughout the year. It caters to all ages, and attracts not only locals but people from all over Britain, Europe and the rest of the world. For all its visitors, it provides physical and spiritual relief from the pressures of modern living, and from the traffic and hubbub of urban life. Its green open spaces, lakes, trees, flowers and birds are an ever more valuable asset.

Although cars – but not trade vehicles – are allowed on the Outer and Inner Circle, walking is and always has been the proper activity in the park. In the morning commuters stride purposefully to work over Primrose Hill, down the Broad Walk or along the park's other axes. Later in the day, other walkers move more slowly, resting at benches or in the cafés; or in the summer sunbathing or sitting on the grass for a picnic. Families with children come out both in the day and in the evenings, at weekends and during the holidays. For lovers, the park and its gardens are ideal places for courtship.

For some a walk is the means of getting from one place to another; for others it is a opportunity to talk and relax; for others still it is a chance to get exercise and fresh air. All shapes and sizes of dogs are to be seen from dawn to dusk, chasing balls and sizing up canine friendships and enmities. Children enjoy the swings, slides and roundabouts in the playgrounds. Joggers and runners of all ages take more strenuous exercise, some using the running track between Macclesfield Bridge and the Zoo (though the track, with its eccentrically narrow ends, does not attract serious runners). Other exercisers are put through routines by their personal trainers or work their way round the open-air gymnasium on Primrose Hill. Although cyclists are banned from most of the park, they have recently been allowed on the Broad Walk; and the Outer and Inner Circles have long provided attractive circuits.

LEFT Deckchairs on the Nannies' Lawn in Queen Mary's Gardens.

RIGHT Walkers make the most of the park's quiet paths, while a lone runner uses the track west of the Zoo and cyclists sweep round the Inner Circle.

BELOW The Royal Horse Artillery rehearsing for a state occasion on Gloucester Green.

BOTTOM The York Bridge tennis courts, on the site of the grounds of the Royal Toxophilite Society, are open to the public.

While private horse-riding is forbidden inside the park, Regent's Park has a long association with horses. The Cart Horse Parade, attracting a thousand entries at its peak, was held on the the Inner and Outer Circles on Whit Monday from 1888. This was complemented from 1904 by the Van Horse Parade on Easter Monday. In 1966 the two amalgamated to form the London Harness Horse Parade, which was held in Regent's Park until 1994. The horses of the Royal Horse Artillery, based in St John's Wood, are also a familiar sight out exercising round the roads of the park in the early morning.

The first official sport in the park was archery. The Royal Toxophilite Society's grounds, on what is now the site of the York Bridge tennis courts, were established in 1832 and lasted until 1922, with the society's distinctive Archers' Lodge on the edge of the boating lake. In winter the grounds were flooded to provide a skating arena that was certainly safer than the boating lake. Since 1922 they have been used as tennis courts open to the public. Boating on the lake, from 1861, at one time included sailing as well as rowing; more

The lake is the principal ornament of the park. Boating on it, in hired boats, has long been a popular activity. There is also a children's boating pond, near Hanover Terrace.

recently pedaloes have been introduced. Primrose Hill offers a ground for boules next to the gymnasium at the bottom of the hill and an outstanding site for kite-flying at its top. When snow falls, Primrose Hill quickly attracts large numbers of children and adults with skis, toboggans, sledges, trays and other improvised means of sliding.

No organized games, or dogs, are allowed in the formal gardens in the park. Pitches for team games in its main body have, however, been another long-term amenity, though until recently limited in the quality of their surfaces by problems presented by the clay soil. Improvements in drainage have now made Regent's Park the largest sports area in central London. A more controversial scheme, to build floodlit, hard-surface, five-a-side football pitches on the site of Holford House, replacing the ninety-year-old Tennis and Golf School there, was defeated in 2008 after widespread protest.

Early in the morning bird-watchers are out looking and listening for the remarkable number of species recorded in the park each year. In the evening, Holme Green is

The park changes almost unrecognizably when the snow settles, bringing with it unusual visitors. Here we see a snow family out for a walk; a snowman making a friend; and a snowman being born in the Avenue Garden. To the right, a snowman takes the weight off his feet; and Primrose Hill becomes an improvised ski resort.

The Diorama. Occupying the central range of Park Square East, the Diorama, designed by Augustus Charles Pugin and James Morgan, seated two hundred patrons in a darkened auditorium. After a fifteen-minute exposure to a 'performance', the auditorium was rotated hydraulically to face a second scene. None of the original machinery survives.

covered by geese and ducks settling down for the night. Throughout the day the Long Bridge offers an opportunity to watch waterfowl and to learn the difference between a mandarin and a Carolina duck. Meanwhile the herons stand around the lake, or on the posts sticking up in it, scanning the water.

The park also offers formal entertainment. The Zoo has continued to attract visitors to the park since it opened in 1828. The Open Air Theatre is a major draw to Queen Mary's Gardens. The park was also at one time home to two other extraordinary places of entertainment. One was the Colosseum, demolished in 1875. The other was the Diorama, an early version of the cinema, filling the three central plots on the east side of Park Square and erected by Jacob Smith in 1823. It had two picture rooms and a revolving auditorium, where visitors were treated to a mixture of projected paintings and sound effects, enhanced by mirrors and magic lanterns. According to the painter John Constable, 'It is in part a transparency, the spectator is in a dark chamber, and it is very pleasing and has great illusion.' The architect and writer James Elmes claimed that

'The delusion is perfect and almost incredible.' Although it was at first extremely successful, the Diorama's appeal soon waned and it was sold for only £3000 in 1848, when it was converted into a Baptist chapel. At one time a rheumatism clinic, it now houses the Prince's Trust. From its early days there have also been displays and events in the park. A variety of shows and festivals have been held in the park in recent years, including flower, food and art fairs.

The original bandstand in the park was near the Readymoney Fountain. In 1930, however, a bandstand was transferred from Richmond Park to Holme Green. Here seven men of the Royal Greenjackets band were killed by an IRA bomb on 20 July 1982. A happier musical association is with the great composer Ralph Vaughan Williams, who lived at 10 Hanover Terrace in the years before his death in 1958. Richard Wagner, who on his visits to London stayed in St John's Wood, fed the ducks from Hanover Bridge and admired the swans on the lake.

The many benches in the park make it a pleasant place to read as well as to talk. As might be expected of such a public space, it has attracted the attention of many authors

Four exhibits at the 2008 Frieze Art Fair:
FAR LEFT The contrarily titled
Pitchfork Colour Blue by Michael Craig Martin;
LEFT *Mind Shut Down* by Supodh Gupta,
made from stainless steel and old utensils;
BELOW   Three of the six sculptures of
Sunrise East by Ugo Rondinone;
BOTTOM *Rectangle Inside Three-Quarter
Cylinder* by Dan Graham.

The bandstand on Holme Green, with weeping willows behind it, rebuilt after the IRA bomb of 23 July 1982. The bomb, which killed seven members of the band of the Royal Green Jackets and injured many of the 120-strong audience, had been hidden beneath the bandstand.

and artists over the years. Among those who have lived around the park are Elizabeth Barrett Browning, Elizabeth Bowen, Charles Dickens, H.G. Wells and Kingsley Amis. Shelley loved to sail paper boats on the now-vanished ponds on Primrose Hill. George Eliot greatly enjoyed the Zoo and Charles Darwin developed an affinity with the orang-utans there. Dante Gabriel and Christina Rossetti lived in Albany Street, as did Edward Lear, who drew many of the birds and animals in the Zoo.

The park today is neither the park that Nash envisaged, nor the park as it was when it was first opened to the public in 1835. Not only have additions been made over the years, there have losses of original buildings and many changes in use. The pressures on the park today are also different from those of the nineteenth century. There are new external threats to its enjoyment. One of the most obvious is the increasing number of high-rise buildings overlooking it. While a view over Regent's Park is clearly a benefit to the developers of these buildings, there is no equivalent benefit to the park itself.

Other questions arise from conflicting priorities over the use of the park. The demand that the park increases the revenue it generates is at times incompatible with its primary purpose, as a refuge from the pressures of the modern world and a place of physical and spiritual recreation. While it is often impossible to reconcile conflicting pressures on the use of a great public asset such as Regent's Park, the contribution its serenity adds to the quality of life of the millions of visitors it attracts each year, something on which it is impossible to put a monetary value, should surely weigh more heavily in the balance than it is sometimes allowed to do.

ACKNOWLEDGEMENTS

I am most grateful to Richard Bowden, Joe Mordaunt Crook, Judy Hillman, Eva Osborne, Valerie St Johnston, Ann Saunders and Geoffrey Tyack for reading this book in draft and making many excellent suggestions for its improvement. I have also profited from the advice of Nick Biddle, John Black, Roger Cline, Tony Duckett, Rosie Hunt, Malcolm Kafetz and Henry Oakeley. I am indebted to Tim Rix, who suggested that I approach Frances Lincoln. This brought me into contact with an exemplary independent publisher: one combining high standards with a personal touch. At Frances Lincoln, I wish to thank Jo Christian, Becky Clarke, Andrew Dunn and John Nicoll. Working with Sandra Lousada, inside and outside Regent's Park, was a pleasure throughout. Finally, I thank my wife, Lucy, for her love and support during the writing of this book and throughout our lives together.

For those who want to know more about the park, Ann Saunders, *Regent's Park* (second edition, London, 1981), remains indispensable, as does John Summerson, *The Life and Work of John Nash, Architect* (revised edition, London, 1980). Michael Mansbridge, *John Nash: A Complete Catalogue* (London, 1991), provides an illustrated guide to Nash's work. For an elegant and erudite lecture on the genesis of the park, see J. Mordaunt Crook, *London's Arcadia: John Nash and the Planning of Regent's Park*, Soane Lecture, 2000 (London, 2001).

The engravings on pages 36, of the Colosseum, and 42–46, showing the early appearance of the villas in the park, are by the topographical artist Thomas Hosmer Shepherd and were published to accompany *Metropolitan Improvements* by the architect James Elmes (1827–28). I am grateful to the following for their kind permission to reproduce illustrations: the Principal, Fellow and Scholars of Jesus College, Oxford, page 12; the National Archives, pages 10 below (MPE1/315), 15 (MEPP 1/58 and CRES 60/2), 16 (CRES 60/3); the City of Westminster Archives Centre, pages 13, 46 below, 60; and the Zoological Society of London, page 87 above.

Bust of John Nash overlooking the garden of Nash House, 3 Chester Terrace. Placed there in 1947 by Lord Gerald Wellesley, later seventh Duke of Wellington, it is a copy of the orginal by William Behnes (1831). As Prime Minister in 1831, the first Duke of Wellington vetoed the award of a baronetcy to Nash.

INDEX